LIBER RUDRA

ASHA'SHEDIM

Copyright 2016 John Putignano
Cover art done by Norman Trinidad
Lilin Society Sigil done by Edgar Kerval

No portion of this book may be reproduced in any form without the written consent of the author, except for brief passages in reviews.

ISBN-13: 978-0997836325
ISBN-10: 0997836326

www.lilinsociety.com

Published by Martinet Press

TABLE OF CONTENTS

PART ONE: MANUSCRIPTS AND RITUALS	6
INTRODUCTION	7
THE AEON OF DARK EMPATHY	8
THE CONCEPT OF SORCERY	13
BLACK SORCERY	14
RITUAL OF THE SEVEN HELLS	16
DEMON SUMMONING RITUAL	17
THE COMMITMENT TO THE SPIRIT OF QAYIN	20
BLOOD SACRIFICE TO BAPHOMET	22
THE ABYSS	24
A BASIC RITUAL FOR GNOSIS	25
APPROVED HUMAN SACRIFICE FOR THE LILIN SOCIETY	27
THE GUIDELINES FOR HUMAN SACRIFICE	28
HUMAN SACRIFICE TO MASTER QAYIN	29
RITUAL OF THE LIVING CAUSAL NEXION	30
THE RITUAL OF EDEN'S APPLE	31
THE SYMBOLISM OF KALI	32
THE SEVEN MANIFESTATIONS OF KALI	33
THE EIGHT MANIFESTATIONS OF BHAIRAVA	38
UNDERSTANDING THE LABYRINTH OF THE LILIN SOCIETY	39
THE PAIN OF EVOLUTION	40
NO PRISONERS	42
BLOOD ORGY TO DARK MOTHER BAPHOMET	43
LESBIAN RITUAL OF THE DEMONIC FEMININE	45
THE LILIN SOCIETY'S BLACK MASS	47
THE NECROSEXUAL RITES OF THE WHORE LILITH	50

SODOMY: A BLASPHEMY FROM THE DEVIL	55
SEXUALITY IN THE LILIN SOCIETY	59
GUIDE TO SEXUAL SORCERY	59
EVIL	61
LIBER INFERNO 2016	62
THE WEAVER 2016	72
THE CLEANSING (ORIGINAL)	76
LIBER LPDLS (ORIGINAL)	78
PART TWO: THE LILIN SOCIETY DRECC	80
INTRODUCTION	81
CODE OF SINISTER HONOUR	81
WHAT IS A DRECC	82
INSIGHT ROLES	83
WHAT IS CAUSAL ABSTRACTION	85
A NEW SATANIST	85
LAWS BASED ON HONOR	87
TEST OF THE POTENTIAL DRECC	88
PART THREE: THE BOOK OF BELIAL	90
THE GODS OF THE ETERNAL WOMB	91
WOMB OF TIAMAT	92
LIBER TWENTY ONE	95
A SINISTER WORLD	96
WEAK SATANISM	97
PREPARATION IN CROSSING THE ABYSS	98
UNDERSTANDING THE NATURE OF THE ABYSS	100
CROSSING THE ABYSS THROUGH CHORONZON	101
GNOSIS OF LILITH-SOPHIA	104
A SACRIFICE TO CHORONZON TO BRING DESTRUCTION	106

LILIN SOCIETY CREED	107
RITUAL TO LEVIATHAN TO BRING DESTRUCTION	108
SATANIC ALCHEMY OF THE BEING	109
REACHING THE LILITH QLIPHA	110
THE CHAVAJOTH	111
PRAYER OF THE DARK CROSSROADS	111
OMOLU PRAYER	112
PRAYER TO CHONRONZON	112
THE TEN HELLS IN SEVEN PLACES	112
THE COSMIC HOLOCAUST	113
AN HONOR TO BELIAL	114
RITUAL TO TANIN'IVER	116
FORMULAS	116
THE HARDSHIPS OF THIS PATH	117
UNDERSTANDING THE ILLUSION	118
PRAISE TO TUBAL CAIN	119
THE SEXUAL RITES OF NAAMAH	119
PART FOUR: FROM INITIATE TO ADEPT	121
INTRODUCTION	122
INITIATION RITUAL	122
INVOKING THE SPIRIT OF QAYIN	123
THE INFERNO PATH	123
ADEPT RITUAL	125
PART FIVE: RUNNING YOUR OWN SECT	127
INTRODUCTION	129
THE SATANIC POINTS	129
LILIN SOCIETY SECT RULES	131
INITIATE TO ADEPT TESTING	132

THE BYLAWS	134
HISTORY OF THE LILIN SOCIETY	135
STRUCTURE	136
CORE BELIEFS OF THE LILIN SOCIETY	137
CONSECRATING THE SACRED TOOLS	139
MEETING OPENING RITUAL	140
MEETING CLOSING RITUAL	141
DEVOTION TO SATAN	141
FUNERAL RITES OF THE LILIN SOCIETY	141
THE MARRIAGE RITES OF THE LILIN SOCIETY	143
INITIATION RITUAL	144
UPON THE DEATH OF A MASTER OR MISTRESS	145
AFTERWARDS	147
PART SIX: BOOK OF INITIATION	148
INTRODUCTION	149
CHAOS	150
THE BOOK OF QAYIN AND LULUWA	152
THE ELEVEN STEPS TO HELL	155
UNDERSTANDING THE ACAUSAL	157
GODDESS OF DEATH	159
OUR SACRED SIGIL	161
THE TEST	162

PART ONE:
MANUSCRIPTS AND RITUALS

INTRODUCTION

What follows are manuscripts. Some are being published for the first time while others have been published before. Many of the old manuscripts have been rewritten for this book. When certain sigils are mentioned but there is no sigil shown such as the Azoth, Nexion, Qayin etc, you are to develop these sigils on your own, crafted during intense meditation. They should be simple and easy to remember. Read on and discover the teachings and wisdom of the Lilin Society.

THE AEON OF DARK EMPATHY

When I formed the Lilin Society back in 2013, it was out of disgust and outrage as to what direction the occult arts had devolved, that lead me towards the infernal path I was to pave. My vision was to seek out like minded Satanists (not weekend Satanists) and form a brotherhood where individuals and sects alike could unite and learn under its umbrella. Our goal since the beginning has been simple yet bold. We seek out the path of internal evolution which can be achieved through Pathei-Mathos.

Pathei-Mathos can be defined as an internal process both individual in nature as well as aeonic. It is learning through adversity; it is wisdom gained through personal suffering and personal experience which all lead to gnosis. Gnosis, or hidden knowledge, is discovered through a combination of personal suffering, adversity, the occult arts and personal experiences both internal and external. If one of these is taken away then the practitioner hasn't reached the requirements to evolve toward gnosis. To understand the limits of the clay prison (flesh) and how minuscule we truly are within the cosmos, will bring us closer to gnosis. It will bring about change.

The Lilin Society thus uses techniques such as insight roles and challenging physical tests to fill the requirements of pathei-mathos. Through ritual sorcery, and especially internal sorcery, we truly learn about ourselves, but only with a combination of other techniques. The Lilin Society may provide a tried and tested path toward enlightenment and evolution to those who wish to commit to our standards. It is the path to gnosis. To slack in one or more areas leads to failure, of delusions of growth, or a false sense of achievement that was not earned. These ignorant beings are unbalanced, absorbed by ego and trade their evolution for an imposter's mask.

With regard to insight roles, there often seems to be confusion as to the purpose they serve. These are roles we willingly take on that purposely place us at odds with ourselves. They are intended to cause inner conflict as well as outer conflict, and thus bring about change and evolution. Becoming a police officer, a right wing fanatic and so forth, are examples of insight roles. I myself have lived the insight role of being the leader of a right wing militia. I supported the Tea Party and took on far right beliefs. My sudden shift confused the people around me, but the role helped me to gain a greater understanding of myself. Once the insight role had served its purpose, I stepped down as General, and the militia has since disbanded. I have also served in the military as a means to achieve insight. This also served as a form of aeonic sorcery, as I supported the killing force that fought muslims, a revolting demiurgic cult. These are but a few examples of how I have used insight roles to foster my own personal development. I view insight roles as a key component in one's personal evolutionary path; these roles are important to me as they should be to everyone within the Lilin Society.

As a Society we strive to surpass the mundane and all limitations bestowed upon the mundanes by the cosmic creator. After our limitations are tried and tested by pathei-mathos, we move to learn to kill our ego, and thus free the Azoth. This is done through fasting, self-mutilation, sleep deprivation, psychedelic drug use, and spiritual segregation. Although these tasks are seemingly trivial, they in fact are detrimental to the development of 'Homo Galacticus', a new human which is more concerned with the internal rather than the external world. This willful shaping and molding of the mind makes us more capable of understanding and receiving gnosis.

We all have the ability to evolve, but it is our contentment within a material world that prevents many of us, especially the mundane, from achieving it. It is our material anchors which tether us to this world and deny us the liberation our spirit strives for: to filter back into timeless chaos. We must break the cycle of rebirth and evolve.

Neophytes within the society often ask me where they should begin. The occult arts can be a labyrinth of possibilities that may confuse one as much as it inspires another. My suggestion is to begin with meditation, for it is meditation that is the root of all successful work. Without a mind detached from the body, the wand and altar are simply material objects without any real power or use. It is the clear mind that communicates with the acausal world which empowers the tools and rituals of Satanism.

Satanists must wrap their mind around the concept of the acausal world, one full of acausal spirits liberated of physical form. Satan is one of many acausal spirits that reside in the other side, but he is simply one of many. A typical misconception is that Satan is the supreme god of chaos, this is not true. The Unknown God is ruler of all cosmic chaos and Satan rules the worlds of Sitra Achra as he looks up to the unmanifested womb to return to chaos.

From this acausal world, we have acausal energies which can be used. This is the true basis of sorcery. The Lilin Society posits that every man and every woman is a nexion to the acausal world. How this is so can be observed through life itself, even within the mundane aspects of materiality. Everything in the universe, from a pencil on a desk, to an asteroid in the sky, needs force to move. This is the cause and effect of the causal world, yet we can move without force simply by thinking it. I tell my arm to move and it does. This is evidence of an outside energy at odds with the causal world within us. We are full of acausal energy and thus we all serve as a nexion to the acausal world. Plants have acausal energy and thus this is why herbal sorcery works. To understand the acausal is to understand sorcery.

Acausal empathy, dark empathy, and sinister empathy are all different terminology describing the sensitivity to (and awareness of) acausal energies. It is beyond causal abstractions, beyond all causal symbols, and beyond occultism, for the occult uses causal symbols and methods to access the acausal. It is thinking in acausal time rather than the cause and effect of causal time.

Acausal beings are beyond our understanding. Some of these acausal beings only exist within the realm of the acausal while others have the means to manifest within this world. These are the demons that we may contact or call upon. They are without physical form but can take a causal form within this world. These beings are beyond morality and causal concepts. It is impossible to hold them to our definition of morality. They exist by their own acausal nature. Acausal beings have the ability to feed off of emotion. They also feed off of energy, such as the prana in blood during a sacrifice (or blood-letting ritual), during the burning of herbs and incense, and so on. They do not live and die for they are eternal.

The examination of the acausal thus brings me to discuss humanity and the causal. Energy can neither be created nor destroyed. Our consciousness is energy. Since it cannot be destroyed, it thus 'lives' forever, surviving the death of the body; it may move toward either the acausal world or may be locked into the vicious cycle of rebirth. Another key word here is created.

The creator god has created our body, created our soul, but our spirit was stolen from this acausal world. It has been imprisoned in this clayform, and in a sense lives in an insight role here in the causal world. This struggle strengthens the spirit as we find gnosis and fight to break the chains of rebirth.

It should also be noted that acausal beings are not restricted by causal travel. Causal travel is physical, and they are not physical beings, and thusly not restricted by the laws of our physical existence. They are all encompassing and everywhere at once. Some are more powerful than others. While some can bring about change within the causal world others cannot, just as some cannot manifest within the causal world.

Here I would like to discuss Baphomet, as there seems to be some confusion over how she is viewed within the Lilin Society. The Lilin Society stands in agreement with the Order of Nine Angles in that Baphomet is the mother of Earth. She is the blood crazing shapeshifter whom has the ability to enter the causal world. It should be noted that this manifestation of Baphomet has nothing to do with the effigy worshipped by the Templars, although we do use this archetypal image since it is so widely identified as Baphomet.

Satan, Baphomet, and the myriad other demons described above are not gods. They are not to be worshipped, feared or obeyed. They are to be admired and respected at all times, but to worship them goes against the law of a Satanist for a Satanist bows before no man nor god. Usage of terms such as 'Lord' and 'Master' are offered out of respect, but do not have a binding restraint to them. We feed them energy and in exchange they thus bring about the change we ask for.

These demons are often considered 'evil', a term which seems to linger around Satanists as a whole. Now this is true in that these demons are void of morals and thus do not uphold the "laws" of human morality. A Satanist is a reflection of these demons, and thus is also 'evil' in this sense. This 'evilness' digs deeper and manifests itself within us as we further delve into aeonic sorcery and sinister acts. We condone and encourage these actions in order to evolve the spirit and fight causal abstractions.

Causal abstractions may be defined as anything man-made or imposed with the purpose of controlling the populace. Everything from government to demiurgic religions should be viewed as causal abstractions. Laws based on morals rather than honor (and the courts which uphold these laws), forced taxation by a state or nation, the education system and all its manipulation, should all be viewed as systems of mind control. These are all tyrannical forms of the demiurge put into the hands of mankind to impose false order. These abominations must be fought, for in order to fully evolve as a populace, we must shed ourselves of causal abstractions. How can we fight the war of the spiritual when the war of the physical stands in our way?

It should be noted that human sacrifice exists within the Lilin Society, but this is performed in a way to prevent the Satanist from going to prison. In the old days, blood was shed before Baphomet and the killer bathed in the blood. Today we must take a more subtle approach to avoid the lengthy jail terms that would restrict us from evolving. We perform all human sacrifice through sorcery, but that is not to say we do it indiscriminately. The art of culling is just that, an art, and the sacrifice must be chosen as a means to benefit Satanism. This is the first task. One must ask "How does the death of this person affect Satanism?" Then the potential sacrifice is tested, tried and finally selected. Our sacrifices are an art and we always adhere to these methods.

In regard to rituals and ceremony the question is often posed as to whether the practitioner can change or add to what has been written for the Lilin Society. Not only is this fine but it is encouraged and expected in order to make the rituals and ceremonies more personalized, and thus more effective. The rituals, the symbols, the steps and so forth are all causal in nature. They are tools to aid us in tapping into the acausal, but they are just that, tools. If you feel, for example, that a step is unnecessary then you may omit it and perhaps replace it with something you feel is more beneficial to yourself. The only requirement is that all rituals performed must adhere to the rules of the Lilin Society in order for them to be used within the umbrella of its name. This is not to say that you may not go beyond the rules (for as we say, rules are causal in nature) but if you choose to do so they are considered solitary rituals which are not to be conducted under our name.

I have received a litany of criticism since the Lilin Society was formed. It seems that many feel that it doesn't need to exist, for Satanism is a solitary path. This is true, but since causal abstractions exist and imposed order exists, and we operate in a causal world, I ask then, what is wrong with uniting like-minded, elite, evolved beings who all wish to learn together and evolve? This anti-social behavior is a product of misanthropy which is a characteristic of the Satanist and although there is nothing wrong with this ideology of hatred, there is also nothing wrong with uniting and working together.

I would like to conclude this essay with a description of the Order of the Dreccs. The Order of the Dreccs is a sub-group built within the Lilin Society. These are individuals devoted to the Laws of the Sinister-Numen. The Sinister-Numen are those who represent types of acausal energy within the causal world. They are sorcerers that have the ability to inspire and influence even the mundanes. Through the Laws of the Sinister-Numen they spread aeonic sorcery to aid in the collapse and overthrowing of any and all causal abstractions. They are a danger to the system, for they are as charismatic as they are dangerous.

The Dreccs blend into society, and purposefully so. They are cops, lawyers, doctors, cashiers, mechanics, etc. Some take insight roles and become political or even religious figures. They appear to contribute to societal order, but it is only a mask that they wear for their true goals are to decimate all causal abstractions. The Dreccs are dissidents willing to fight this Earthly battle through physical action, deception and aeonic sorcery.

The path of the Drecc is a solitary path, even more so than that of a typical Satanist. Dreccs do not know about one another. Many people don't even know that they are Satanists, but just exist as such. There are no Drecc meetings or get-togethers. The Drecc is a Lilin Society member, but within the Lilin Society their Drecc status is a secret.

A good example of a Drecc engaging in an insight role is to become a catholic priest. To the community the deception is real and from within the church he will cause havoc and chaos. When the chaos comes to fruition, no one will suspect the Drecc, for he is a good actor and plays his part well. If the Drecc's insight role involves him marrying a mundane to keep the role going, he will not fall in love with her. He will in secret raise his children to be Satanists and once the role is over he will divorce his mundane wife. Not everyone is cut out to be a member of the Lilin Society, and not every member is cut out to be a Drecc. Only the elite among the elite will live this lifestyle, and the reward of spreading the sinister will be well deserved.

THE CONCEPT OF SORCERY

Sorcery, in this context, is a system that brings about change in an individual, whether it is internal (sorcery creating change within the individual) or external (sorcery creating change within the causal). If one does not change, then the sorcery was in vain. Sorcery is applied through practical means in the causal world (ritual, tools etc) and the end result is acausal change either internally or externally. The more connected to the acausal world the sorcerer is, the greater his success will be and the less he will need practical means to achieve this.

Sorcery has the potential to create great insight and thus a further understanding of self, others and the world. Sorcery returns the individual to their inner self by destroying illusion. Aeonic sorcery comes in many forms. This is where sorcery is applied throughout a populace over a period of time to cause change in the minds of that populace. This aim of aeonic sorcery is to bring about an evolution or destruction of the mundane populace. Grand culling is a form of aeonic sorcery. War, terrorism and even the government manufactured AIDs virus are all forms.

The AIDS virus was manufactured by the causal abstractions of government as a purging of a segment of the populace, primarily targeting blacks, gays and the poor. It was introduced to the populace through hepatitis B experiments performed on gay and bisexual men between 1978-1981. Today the AIDs virus has expanded so fast that it now indiscriminately attacks the entire populace without mercy. The plan of genocide back fired against causal abstraction, however, we now are left with a genocidal aeonic culling on a mass level.

Eventually, as a Sorcerer, you will hit a wall. This wall is the limit you can work unless you face Choronzon and cross the abyss. All sorcerers will face this challenge one day if they wish to continue on their ascension, but understand the real danger of this. Only well trained adept minds should even attempt to cross the abyss for only terror and insanity await those not ready.

BLACK SORCERY

Often I try not to use the word "magic" and I avoid the term "magick" at all costs. These words have been taken by society and pulverized. Black Sorcery needs to have a fear to it, a fear in the eyes of the spiritless Clayborn. This is no longer achievable with the word magic, but sorcery has still kept its edge.

Black sorcery is not a means to play around with. The Weekend Satanists and healers of the world will find only terror and possibly death within the dark arts. It takes a properly trained mind to comprehend, let alone deploy such arcane acts.

There are three forms of sorcery and these are external, internal and Aeonic. The first one is external sorcery, meaning changing the causal world around you. The second form, acausal, is internal sorcery. It is changes that happen from within. The final form, Aeonic, is the most threatening. They affect mass groups of people over a period of time. This is the manipulation of the mindless, the forced change of consciousness. It is bending the will and beliefs of all those around you in order to achieve a Satanic agenda.

Crystals should always be employed in sorcery. Many shun at this because of the popularity of them among the pagan and Wiccan communities, but understand that the crystal responds to voice vibration and thus acts as an amplifier to which thought is able to be transmuted into actual sorcery.

Now it is understood that man is divided into three categories. There are the Hyletic which are ruled by body, the Psychic which are ruled by soul and the pneumatic which are ruled by spirit. They are also known as the Pasu which are animals, the Vira which are warriors striving to wake, and Divya which are the liberated spirits.

The Hyletic will never get sorcery to work, nor can they even comprehend it. That is why so many people turned it into a modern joke and label it superstition, for much of this world descends from the spiritless Adam rather than the Fireborn Qayin.

Now I mentioned earlier that we all are nexions containing acausal energy. Do not misunderstand this to mean that all humans have the spirit, Azoth. These are two different things. Once this concept of nexion and acausal energy is understood it can be employed though the act of sorcery. This explains a lot of the "super natural" entities and events which do not seem to correlate with a causal realm.

As dark sorcerers we study, employ and learn with black sorcery in all forms and from all traditions. Witchcraft transcends religion. What works for the Sumerian witches will work for the Ancient Egyptian witches and shall work for us. The sorceries of Voodoo, Quimbanda, Macumba, Santa Muerte...they all worked for their people and now shall work for us. We just need the understanding, the ritual and the will.

The other kind of Sorcery involves death. A Satanist must be ready to die. If he has not completed his work within the causal world then he can transfer his spirit to another human being, by doing this he retains his knowledge which is often lost in the death/ rebirth cycle by the means of retaining his ego. This is not something learned over night. It takes years of learning and developing a strong spirit and the rituals to do this take long periods of time with multiple sorceries. A crystal tetrahedron should be used during this. Both the transfer and accepting vessel must be present to complete as the stronger spirit invades and conquers that of the lesser spirit or spiritless.

If the sorcerer is ready and he has achieved all he wants from this world then he can prepare his spirit to leave this world and enter its new home in the acausal. The first step to this is limiting life anchors, the distractions which chain our spirit to the death/rebirth cycle. This involves a detachment from the world, spiritual segregation, a loathing for this world and internal sorcery. A sorcerer cannot simply up and decide one day that they are ready, they must work on it all their life and open that doorway. Conquer your indulgences and abstain.

A Satanist does not die weak and feeble. He dies strong and ready to die. He dies long after he kills his ego and only when he is ready to die. Those who waste their life studying the occult and not applying it have done nothing but wasted a lifetime.

In the end the real Satanist will see the glory of Satan and the magnificent lawlessness of the other side. The main goal of life is to return to the Other Side and unite with the Unmanifested Universe.

RITUAL OF THE SEVEN HELLS

Seven black candles surround the practitioner in a circle. At each candle is a sacrificial animal, a goblet of wine, and a bowl. Burning on the altar is 3 parts cinquefoil,v3 parts chicory root and one part clove which has been ground together on a Wednesday. Working counterclockwise light each candle saying the name of the hell at that candle. The names are

1. Sheol
2. Abbadon
3. Bar Shachath
4. Tit ha-Yon
5. Shaare Moth
6. Tzelmoth
7. Gehenna

Now return to the first candle and kill your sacrifice with an obsidian blade. Pour the blood in the bowl and some of the blood in the wine. At each candle say the translation of the seven hell's names as follows:

1. Abyss
2. Destruction
3. Pit of Ruin
4. Mire of Mud
5. Gatesof Death
6. Shadow of Death
7. Valley of Hinnom

and then return to the center of the circle and meditate. Chant the word "Arqa". Envision descending down the seven hells and achieving gnosis as you pass each one.

Now return to the first candle and drink the wine, repeating the name of the Hell. When you finish the wine pour the blood from the bowl onto the candle to extinguish the flame. Make your way around and when you are complete and all candles extinguished return to the center and say "In the name of Lord Satan, it is done."

Now bury these candles in seven different graves all parallel to each other. They should be in a graveyard with a church and seven rows down from the church.

DEMON SUMMONING RITUAL

The ceremony, the sacrifice, the incantations…every part of this ritual are equally important and the whole process tends to be a long and exhausting task. First a circle is declared. This circle is to be used to house all the energy being used.

Commanding a spirit to show itself is the last step and it should be avoided fully. We are not chaining these spirits to the names of cosmic order and creation, however if one must force them to show themselves then by all means do so.

We start off this ritual with the circle which is done as follows.

Earth "Lirach tasa vefa wehlic, Belial"
Air "Renich tasa uberaca biasa icar, Lucifer"
Fire "Ganic tasa fubin, Flereous"
Water "Jedan tasa hoet naca, Leviathan"

The circle will be as follows.

The hendecagram represents the eleven anti cosmic demons of the Chavajoth. In the center is the sigil of Lucifer. The pitchfork represents the mind, body and spirit of the practitioner and it is at the end of this pitchfork where the demon should manifest whether it be through a scrying mirror, flame etc. The altar with all the tools should be within the circle and at each angle a black candle should be lit. There should be no artificial light nor day light within the room.

The practitioner can have an assistant if he wishes but he must remain quiet during the ritual and never leave the circle. The practitioner will now use chalk to draw the sigil of the demon he is summoning at the top of the pitchfork. If he does not know the sigil one should be made one week prior, constructed by meditating upon the name of the spirit and all energy should be focused into this sigil. The sigil must be kept in a black box when not being used however it should be handled during meditation as much as possible.

The sigil is also drawn on parchment paper along with the name of the spirit. This is placed in a black box with some sulfur and asafoetida. The box is then wrapped in iron. This will be used for the command if nothing else works.

Open the ritual with a basic chant. I suggest the Diablous chant. This is as follows.

> "Dies irae, dies illa
> Solvet Saeclum in favilla
> Teste Satan cum sibylla.
> Quantos tremor est futurus
> Quando Vindex est venturus
> Cuncta stricte discussurus.
> Dies irae, dies illa!"

Next you will recite an opening prayer to Lucifer.

> "Lord Lucifer, anti cosmic bringer of Light
> bringer of Gnosis and truth
> I am devoted to you and call into the acausal realms
> I call forth a spirit
> May you help me in reaching this spirit
> Hail Lucifer"

Next you will light incense appropriate to your spirit. You will chant "Chav-a-joth" while circling the circle eleven times. Then you will use your wand and draw the sigil of the demon in the sky. You will recite the following conjuration.

> In the name of Lord Lucifer, I call you _____

I call to you to appear to before me
I ask that you take a form I can understand
In the name of Lucifer and the Chavajoth
I call you here now _____

You will now perform your sacrifice. Take a vigin, young and healthy black colored animal and slice its throat so that it cannot shriek and waste its energy. Let the blood flow onto the floor and collect some of it in your hands. Take the blood and drink from your hands and then raise your hands high and recite the following.

"I spill this blood in the name of Lucifer and in the name of _____"

If the spirit doesn't come repeat two or three times. Each time you should increase your pitch and ferocity of how you speak. If this doesn't work recite the following incantation.

In the name of Lucifer I command you_____to appear before me.
I call to you and command you to take a form I can understand.
In the name of Lucifer and the Chavajoth
I command you now! Manifest Before Me!

If this hasn't brought the spirit to you after three commands it is time to commit to more drastic measures. Light a fire outside the circle where the pitchfork ends and take the box with the sigil. Place it at the end of your sword and raise it above the flames.

Spirit, _____ I command you to come to me now!
In the name of Lucifer and the Chavajoth
I command your presence now!

Now you will drop the box into the flames. If the spirit appears then you are to extinguish the flame. Anytime the spirit arrives be polite yet firm. Do not be humble but be careful not to offend it.

When you are done with the spirit you will thank him and bid him farewell. Once the spirit has left the chamber the ritual has been completed. Meditate and reflect upon your work and document it all in a journal.

THE COMMITMENT TO THE SPIRIT OF QAYIN

This ritual will take one week and take place in the wilderness. Hike for three hours before settling on a place and then create an earthen altar. On this altar one should have human bones, black and red candles, roses and a crown of thorns.

Set up your tent.

You will start the ritual during the planetary hour of Mars. Strip naked and bring out your animal sacrifice. Slice its throat with an obsidian blade and pour the blood on the altar.

Raise the obsidian blade to the sky and recite.

> "In the name of Qayin, Lord of Death, I begin this ritual of commitment. Accept my blood sacrifice. In the name of Satan, hail the spirit of the first murderer."

Now meditate for an hour. Reflect on the story of Qayin and Luluwa. When you are done return to your tent and sleep for three hours.

The ritual will consist of seven full days. Each day will be the same with the exception of the last day. On each day you will follow the ritual described.

Wake up and eat a light breakfast. Drink plenty of water. Ritualistically bathe and during the bath light frankincense. The bath water should have rose petals in it. You do not need a bath tub just a bowl with water. Around the bowl should be human bones and animal bones to form a circle. Take four knives and stick a knife in the ground at the North, East, South and West points.

After the bath get dressed and meditate for a hour facing the altar. Chant the word Qayin while focusing on your Azoth.

Rise and with your obsidian blade draw the sigil for Qayin before you and the Symbol of Azoth above you.

> "I stand before this altar as I shed my ego and free my Azoth. I stand before the spirit of Qayin and invoke the spirit to bind with my own. In the name of Satan, Hail the first Murderer!"

Now walk forward into the sigil of Qayin and concentrate. Focus all his energy into your body as you envision him combining with your spirit.

Go on a four hour hike not stopping to rest. Drink plenty of water during this but do not eat food. Bring with you a human bone and an animal skull. Bring also a small shovel as well as four black candles, the obsidian blade and a rose. Also bring parchment and a pen.

After the hike you will find a clearing. Here you will dig a six foot hole and place the animal skull and human bone in it. Around it place the four candles in the four directions (north, south, east and west) and stand in the grave. Raise the obsidian knife and call out to the sky.

> "In the name of Qayin I did this grave. I call upon the Lord of Death to enter my body and empower me. Bring me closer to Gnosis."

Now meditate in the grave for one hour, focusing on the bones. On the parchment draw the sigil of Qayin and place it on top of the bones. Climb out of the hole and bury the bones and parchment. On top of the grave mound place some rose pedals. Turn around and hike back to camp without looking back.

At the camp you will read about Qayin. You will reflect on what Qayin is and what you hope to achieve by binding and committing to him. You will then walk around the camp clockwise seven times chanting Qayin.

Sacrifice an animal before the earthen altar and spill the blood on the altar. Raise the blade and announce "In the name of Qayin!"

Spend the rest of the day in reflection and meditation. Sleep no more than three hours.

The purpose of this ritual is to weaken the body and strengthen the spirit. You are to exhaust yourself by eating once a day and going through physical tasks.

On the last day after completing all the following before going to bed you will stand before the altar naked. You will recite.

> "Master Qayin, Lord of Death, First Murderer, I call you here now. I have committed myself to you, committed my spirit to you, and ask you to bind with my spirit to bring me closer to Gnosis. In the name of Satan, I make this sacrifice."

Now use the obsidian blade to slice open your left palm. Spill the blood on the crown of thorns. Meditate for one hour and then raise the crown above your head and chant the word Qayin as you place it upon your head.

Go to sleep while wearing the crown for no more than three hours and in the morning pack up camp, leaving behind the earthen altar and all its contents with the exception of the crown. Wear this crown during your hike back into the world. Once you arrive at your destination (where you began your initial hike) you can remove the crown. When you get home place it upon your altar.

BLOOD SACRIFICE TO BAPHOMET

Baphomet is the Blood Mother of Sacrifice and Sexuality. This ritual is a human sacrifice ritual involving blood and orgy. This ritual is done in a group setting in a woods. This ritual is a devotion to the spirit of Baphomet and all she represents. It is vital that the human sacrifice requirements are met in order to conduct this ritual for this is a ritual that advances Satanism. The Master and Mistress will test and decide on the human sacrifice.

For one week each participant will make a daily sacrifice on their own to the spirit of Baphomet. This is done in the following way.

Stand in the center of the room facing the statue or image of Baphomet. Hold the sacrifice out in one hand and proclaim in your own words your devotion to Satan, Satanism and the spirit of Baphomet. The sacrifice is killed with an obsidian blade and the blood is collected in a bucket. Each day for seven days you will add blood to this bucket.

On the seventh day go to a clearing and agree on a planetary hour to work in. There should be a Master and Mistress (leaders one of which is male and the other female). Together these two are a representation of the male and female aspects of Baphomet and should be treated as holy during the ritual as if they are Baphomet.

There will be an altar with a Baphomet image on it and nothing else.

The participants file in chanting Baphomet in order of male, female, male etc. They are wearing black robes and nude underneath. Each robe should have a pentagram on the left side of the breast. It can be painted on or sewn on. Once they reach the clearing they will form a circle still in the male, female structure. At the foot of each will be a bucket of blood, a chalice and a candle.

All will be silent and the Master and Mistress will enter the circle.

Master: We are gathered here to celebrate and devote ourselves to the spirit of Baphomet.

Mistress: We invoke the spirit within us and celebrate with blood sacrifice as well as a human sacrifice.

Master: In the name of Lord Satan we summon the darkness and through the art we celebrate the spirit of Baphomet. A spirit of blood sacrifice and sexuallity.

Mistress: Hail Satan

All: Hail Satan

Now all will disrobe in their nude form. Each participant will stand still and chant Baphomet as the Master and Mistress go to each chalice, pouring in red wine. In the center the Master and Mistress will raise their wine glasses, cross arms and drink their wine. The participants will follow, drinking the glass without crossing arms. The Master and Mistress will now disrobe. On their bodies (abdomen) will be painted in blood a pentagram. Each participant will now use their finger and use the blood in the bucket to draw a pentagram on their body.

Each member will now pick up their bucket of blood and in a circle pass the altar, dumping the blood on the altar, directly onto the image of Baphomet. When the blood spilling is complete the Master and Mistress will do the same.

> Master: We have chosen a human sacrifice for this event. His name is _____ and his death will benefit Satanism. In the name of Satan I offer up this sacrifice.

The Master will then place a poppet on the altar. The poppet has a picture of the sacrifice. He will plunge an obsidian blade into the poppet and all will say "Hail Satan"

The Master and Mistress will now engage in sex upon the altar. The participants will now also engage in sexual activity. If the participant is a homosexual or a lesbian they may use a member of the same sex. The orgy happens in the center of the circle with all members in close proximity of each other.

The orgy is finished when the Master and Mistress finish. Right before the Master ejaculates the Mistress will remove the penis from her vagina and use her hand to finish him, ejaculating onto the image of Baphomet.

Once this is complete all will robe and file out male, female etc. while chanting Baphomet. The Master and Mistress will follow last and no one will look back or visit the area again.

THE ABYSS

The abyss is where the causal and acausal meet and intersect. We each have, deep in our subconscious, the abyss. This is because everyone is a nexion to the acausal realm. This is where we come from, this is where our spark was stolen from and thus it is our connection to it. One can go their entire life totally unaware that the abyss exists unless they look for it. Our ego blocks it, the illusionary light cast by the Demiurge. So how does one discover the abyss; through acausal sorcery.

The Wrathful Gods look for ways into our world to destroy it. If we seek the abyss the Wrathful Gods will help us to evolve to the point where we can access it. This abyss is similar to the Tehiru where the thoughtful and thoughtless light divided into two sides. Within all of us is a Tehiru.

So how does one access the abyss, their own Tehiru? The first step is spiritual segregation. This is remaining away from all contact, human or otherwise, for a set period of time. Usually a day or two will suffice as you break down your ego's need to attach itself to this world and delve deep into your own mind to break down the ego and the physical body.

During this segregation one will not eat. They will drink the minimum it takes to survive and they will not toy with any earthly aspects which includes technology or even books. Refrain from any sort of masturbation. This is a time for you and your thoughts.

Next you will walk for an undetermined amount of time. When you are exhausted set up camp and prepare for the ritual. On the ground draw an eleven angle sigil with the wand.

At each point put a black candle and light it. Envision the sigil glowing red, then purple and then back to red. Stand in the center of the sigil and envision yourself stepping into the abyss. Envision the acausal realm the best you can comprehend it.

Trace a circle in the sky above you, then trace one in the air below you.

"I open the ways of the abyss. Let me be a conduit for which the acausal energies of lawlessness and chaos can flow through this human nexion. Allow me time in the abyss, allow me time with my Azoth. Gods of the Other Side, I call to you all in your wrathful forms."

Now draw a pitchfork in front of you with the wand. In the center of the pitchfork start making a never completing circle which grows and shrinks, much like a spiral. As this spiral continues chant "Open the gates. Chaos" Do this several times.

Take the blood letting knife and cut open your wand hand. Grip the wand in a bloody fist. Raise the wand high and conduct the pitchfork/spiral/chant several times. Then lower the want to the air below you and conduct again the pitchfork/spiral/chant.

With your other hand hold and raise the quartz tetrahedron to eye level and gaze deep inside of it. Chant the word "Chaos". Your body is now weak with hunger, thirst, deprived of causal contact and blood loss. This is you killing your ego, your suicide to free the Azoth so that you may enter the Abyss.

Hold the crystal and go to all four directions and above and below and trace a pentagram with the wand in each direction, all while looking into the quartz.

When done recite "I open the gate to the abyss. I welcome the acausal energies and the form they may take."

Chant more as images begin to form within the crystal. If you see images then you have entered the abyss. If you are ready enlightenment nears, but if you are not you will face pure terror and maybe even death.

Repeat chants as many times as you can while gazing into the quartz. This could take hours or even days without a break. When you cannot take any more you may lower the crystal and spend the next hour in deep meditation. After this the ritual is complete. You leave the room, leaving the nexion open.

A BASIC RITUAL FOR GNOSIS

We start with the eleven angle sigil. This symbolizes the wrathful gods of cosmic chaos. This symbol is drawn in chalk on the ground, if outside it can be drawn on cloth and laid on the ground or drawn with corn starch. The eleven points each have a black candle. These are lit prior to the ritual.

All altar setups are to be cleansed with a few drops of grain alcohol prior to use. If you cannot acquire grain alcohol regular alcohol will work. The altar setup should have what is necessary to perform the ritual you are about to conduct. Suggestions are to include incense, candles appropriate to ritual, statues appropriate to ritual, personal sigil, sigils appropriate to ritual and the tools.

Seven red candles will be placed in front of altar. They are lit prior to ritual. At each candle place a glass which is empty. Light the appropriate incense and call forth the spirit you wish to work with. We will use Naamah for this example.

"By the wrathful gods of the Anti-Cosmos, by the Chavajoth and by Lord Satan, I invoke you Naamah. By nightside of Sitra Achra and by the nameless god of Ur-Chaos, I ask you here to this altar, I ask you to come before this temple of flesh and ask you to appear before me. I now will send an offering." Now in each glass pour alcohol (wine is best) and place a cigar on the top lip of each glass. Light a cigar and puff it while circling the eleven fold sigil. Puff the smoke and exhale it inward. Get yourself into a trance. Repeat a mantra while circling. Start off loud and get softer and faster as you go on. Make eleven revolutions and then stop in the center. Puff the cigar and place it on the ground. Take a position and meditate.

Continue with your mantra of choice until you are in a deep meditated state. When you reach this state repeat in your head:

"Naamah, I offered you gifts of this planet. I now offer you blood."

Stand up and exit the sigil. Make eleven revolutions around the sigil while puffing the cigar and continue with your mantra. Place the Cigar on the altar in front of the black mirror. Retrieve the sacrificial animal and bring it to the center of the sigil. Stab it and let the blood spill out in the center. Stand and retrieve the wand. Trace in the air the eleven angle sigil while saying out loud. Darkest spirits I invoke, the darkness of chaos. I stand before the gates of Sitra Achra. This animal was sacrificed to feed your bloodlust, now I ask that you possess this body and help me get past the ego, to dig deep inside myself and find the gnosis hidden by the demiurge. By the Chavajoth, by Lord Satan and by Ur-Chaos I ask you to enter my body and enlighten me in the name of the nameless god of Chaos.

Return to the center of the room and meditate while staring into a black mirror.

All gifts (wine, sacrifice, blood, cigars) are buried eleven feet deep and a cloth is buried on top with the eleven angle sigil. A black candle is placed on top of the gifts. Turn and walk away without looking back.

APPROVED HUMAN SACRIFICE FOR THE LILIN SOCIETY

The Lilin Society does have an approved human sacrifice ritual. Before we get into this let us first discuss the purpose of a human sacrifice. The death of an individual in the name of Satanism releases this sacrifices energy which can be stored within a crystal or spread throughout the causal world. This spreading strengthens the nexion into the acausal world much as it did when Qayin and Luluwa sacrificed Abel and Aklia.

Our human sacrifice guidelines are built upon those taught by the Order of the Nine Angles. First we must discuss the kind of human sacrifices that exist.

The first one is a willing sacrifice. This person has become so overcome with misanthropy and detached from the causal world that they are ready to journey back to the acausal. By shedding their clayform they kill their ego and thus free the energy of it, which can and will be harvested.

The second type is the involuntary sacrifice. This person has no desire to die and is chosen because they stand as an insult to Satanism. They are an opponent and their eradication is for the best. Their energy is now free to use in the hands of those who know what to do with it.

The third type is a result of events. This can range from mass murders, serial murders, acts of terrorism or even war. This human sacrifice happens daily and the energy is often wasted. The demiurge shuns the murder of his creations so all murders are satanic in nature.

There are three methods one can go about sacrificing an individual. The first method is through dark sorcery. This method is employing various death rituals that strike at the sacrifice. Energy is used to do your bidding and often animal sacrifice is a part of this ritual to strengthen the energy.

The second method is through direct contact with the individual. This is done in a ritual setting in which the sacrifice is brought to a ritual area to be sacrificed physically with a sacrificial obsidian knife. The body is then taken and disposed of, special care that it is not discovered by authorities.

The third and final method is that of assassination. Targeting a person and acting as a lone wolf. These methods are carried out usually in a professional manner. The JFK assassination, Martin Luther King, Abraham Lincoln and Osama Bin Laden are all examples of Satanic human sacrifices carried out in this manner.

The second and third method are not condoned by the Lilin Society. The only approved Human Sacrifice is that of method number one. All members of a Human Sacrifice ritual are sworn to secrecy. They will not talk about it, write about it, or in any way let those not involved with the ritual know about it. To break this oath is punishable through death using the first method.

THE GUIDELINES FOR HUMAN SACRIFICE

Human sacrifice is an important ritual for the Satanist, as well as the Lilin Society. I have adopted and modified the Order of the Nine Angles guidelines for human sacrifice.

When a proper sacrifice is found one must not be blinded by personal agenda. If someone wronged you this will not be a proper sacrifice. A sacrifice to Satan must benefit Satanism in some way, not you as a person. If someone insulted you, how does their death benefit Satanism as a whole? It doesn't, and thus it is not a proper sacrifice.

Sacrifices are important for they help thin weak and poisoned human stock. It weeds out the excess and makes room for more enlightened souls. No member of the Lilin Society will be sacrificed unless they have broken some sort of oath and have become a blemish on Satanism. The sick dog will then be sacrificed, with the Grand Council's approval.

A victim will be selected on the grounds that they are a hinder on the advancement of Satanism or that their sacrifice would benefit Satanism in some way. Will their death aid the cause of Satanism?

The victim must be tested and by this they must prove that their death is worthy of a Satanic sacrifice. The testing methods must be decided by those bringing the sacrifice to the table and sufficient evidence must be submitted to the Grand Council before a decision can be made. Understand that our sacrifices are not chosen at random like our animal sacrifices. The death must mean something.

Satanic human sacrifice must glorify Satan, reflect our values in that it aids in evolution in a positive way and must aid in the advancement of the participants and the Lilin Society.

HUMAN SACRIFICE TO MASTER QAYIN

WARNING: This ritual contains a human sacrifice that does not adhere to the laws of the Lilin Society. This ritual is no longer used in the Lilin Society and is only being posted for educational reasons. The author is not responsible for those who misuse the content within this publication.

Master: Scythe bearer come and reap the acausal energy from this body. May I feel your scythe within my flesh, between my bones and buried in my viscera. Master Qayin, Lord of Death, bring pestilence upon my ego and free my Azoth from its prison. Behold, great first murderer, we offer you this sacrifice in your honor. Lord of Death, accept this corpse and bring it to Euronymous so that he may feed upon it until nothing is left but the energy in spilt prana. We've prepared the funeral, and now we give you the offering"

The sacrifice is brought out. The sacrifice should be a woman of child bearing age. She must be naked with the mark of Qayin drawn upon her abdomen. The mark must be in red ink. The sacrifice must be beautiful with voluptuous breasts, a thin frame, child bearing hips and a well shaped rear for only the best will do for our master. She will be tied down upon the altar with black ropes. To the left and right of her head will be black candles and between her thighs right below her vagina will be a red candle.

Take out the virgin cloth (this is a cloth made from the skin of a virgin animal) and place it upon the face of the sacrifice. The participants now approach the altar while chanting Qay-in.

The master raises a human skull which represents spirit free of the flesh prison. He then continues: "Lord of Death, first murderer, first gravedigger, father of all witchcraft; we ask now that you accept this sacrifice."

The Master will now lower the skull onto the table. He will take the red candle and spill wax from the candle onto the sacrifices vagina. The painful screams will echo the room and put the Master in a trance. He places the candle down to retrieve the obsidian blade. He will raise it high.

Master: "Master Qayin, with this blade I shall end the life of this sacrifice. I shall free her from this illusion and may her prana satisfy your blood thirst."

The Master will bring the obsidian blade down with all his might, breaking through the rib cage and entering the blade into the heart of the sacrifice. The Master will now remove the virgin cloth from the face of the sacrifice. He will remove the obsidian blade and use the blade of the knife to remove her eyes and tongue. He must do this fast for this needs to be done before she dies.

Once the sacrifice has died the master will climb on top of the corpse. He will sit on the corpse's chest in his chosen Asana and meditate while holding in his left hand the eyes and tongue of the sacrifice which rest in the virgin cloth. The participants will chant Qay-In during this. The Master will now reach down and retrieve a crown of thorns. He will place it upon his head.

After the ritual the eyes and tongue remained wrapped in the virgin cloth and are buried in a graveyard. The body of the sacrifice will be burned after each participant has been given a chance to meditate on top of it.

RITUAL OF THE LIVING CAUSAL NEXION

This ritual consists of the practitioner using his own body to channel acausal energy using himself as a nexion to the acausal world. The practitioner will go into a state of spiritual and physical segregation for the period of one day. During this time the practitioner will have no access with the outside world. He will spend his time in reflection and meditation. He will fast and he will not sleep.

The next day the practitioner arise from a meditated position. He will say a prayer to Satan while kneeling upon broken glass. He will then strip naked and bath his body in warm water with thyme, lavender, acacia, borage, graveyard dirt from a fresh grave and blood from a day old sacrifice. The sacrifice must be of a black animal in which the throat was slit and blood collected in a chalice. The practitioner will light lotus incense and seven black candles which surround the bath tub. While bathing he will recite a mantra of his choice.

After the bath is complete he will put on only a black ceremonial robe and shoes. He will bring with him a bag with the following items; scrying mirror, wand, incense, seven black candles, Baphomet statue, altar cloth, dagger, and spiritual journal. He will enter the wilderness hiking for one hour. Once he reaches a clearing the practitioner will set up his altar directly upon the Earth.

"Lord Satan, ruler of Sitra Achra, I declare my intentions to use my body as a nexion to the acausal world. I ask that you be my guide during this ritual and allow me access to the acausal energy from the other side. Hail Satan"

Now he will light the seven candles and incense. The practitioner raises the wand and draws the sigil of the nexion above him. He closes his eyes and kneels before the altar and kisses the statue of Baphomet.

"Blood mother Baphomet, bride of Satan, guide me to the acausal."

He takes the dagger and cuts open his left and right palms. He holds his arms over the statue and lets the blood spill upon it. He envisions the prana empowering the statue and satisfying the Blood Mother. He chants "Ba-pho-met" while gazing into the scrying mirror. He will envision the acausal energy as a red light descending from above and into his body. He feels its warmth coming over him. He must ignore his body's aches and other distractions of the body as he lets it become a nexion. This should go on for about an hour. After this the practitioner says a personal closing prayer and writes down all he saw and felt. He is to return home and spend one more day in isolation. The next day the ritual is complete.

THE RITUAL OF EDEN'S APPLE

Enter the chamber chanting "chaos". When you get to the altar pick up your wand and draw the sigil of Azoth in the sky in front of you. Behind you draw the sigil of ego. In the sky above you draw a circle with the nexion inside of it. Below you draw a circle and the sigil of the abyss.

"Before me is my spirit. This is my true self. This is my Azoth. Behind me is the dreaded chains of the Demiurge in the form of my ego. They have leached onto my Azoth and drain it of vitality. I open the nexion to Sitra Achra above me and channel the acausal energy through me and into the abyss. In the name of Samael-Lilith and the eleven acausal demons of the Chavajoth I seek out enlightenment and Gnosis. I seek the means to evolve."

Now sacrifice your animal offering and pour blood into eleven bowls which form a circle around you. Near each bowl light a black candle and take a moment to pray to that demon of the Chavajoth. Now walk the inner circle eleven times while chanting chav-a-joth.

Return to the center before the altar and sit in a comfortable asana. Get yourself into a trance by chanting a mantra of your choice. Envision energy coming from each bowl, the prana of the sacrifice mixed with the acausal energy of the demons. Envision it taking the likeness of ethereal hands reaching out to you, grabbing you and absorbing into you. Envision the color of this energy as being a crimson red as you absorb it into your head (nexion) and let it run down your body and exit your feet (abyss).

Do not envision the abyss for this is dangerous for the inexperienced, those not ready to see the abyss. Instead envision the starvation and weakening, the killing of the ego. Picture it as a rotting corpse full of maggots as the earth elements of Belial eat away at it. Picture the great Euronymous feasting on the corpse of your ego in a banquet. Now look deep into your Azoth.

Lift the amulet of Azoth (a piece of wood with the sigil of Azoth carved, burnt or painted on) and raise it to your lips. Perform a mantra letting the words vibrate off the wood. Envision tapping into the collective consciousness.

Once finished stand and envision the energy flow stopping. You should feel weak, lethargic, maybe even depressed. Now chant and circle the inside of the circle eleven times, blowing out the candle at each bowl on the eleventh rotation, stopping to say a prayer to that demon. Retrace the sigils with the wand in the opposite direction and order from where you began and retrieve the crystal which sat on the altar. Keep this crystal on your body for one week chanting and scrying into it regularly.

THE SYMBOLISM OF KALI

In Hindusim there is ultimately one and that is Devi although she takes on many different forms to allow us to comprehend her. Her most powerful is that of Kali. Even Kali has many manifestations which will be discussed later.

Her blackness is an absence of color and this represents that Kali is absolute reality, beyond the illusion set by the Demiurge. This represents her ability to transcend all manifestations.

In her nakedness she is free from all covering of the Demiurge's illusion. She is illuminated by the light beyond creation and exists in consciousness beyond ego. She is gnosis exposed among the illusion of creation.

Her garland of fifty human heads symbolizes knowledge and wisdom. Her girdle of human hands signify the action of the cosmic laws of Karma and that the wheel of Karma is demolished by those who devote to Kali. Thus Kali is absolute freedom in this world of creation, absolute freedom among the illusion. She demolishes the wheel of Karma.

Her darting red tongue is symbolic of tasting all the forbidden fruits which we are denied in this world of illusion. She enjoys the flavors and is absolute indulgence.

Her four arms represent the complete cycle of creation and destruction. All creation will one day come to an end and the spirit will be liberated. Her right hands represent her creative aspect while the left hands represent her destructive aspect. The bloody head and sword she carries symbolizes the dawn of gnosis, a cosmic understanding that will liberate the spirit from the shackles of ego. The sword of knowledge cuts through the illusion and destroys false consciousness. Her three eyes are the sun, moon and fire in which she sees the past (sun) present (moon) and future (fire, the great cosmic holocaust).

Kali resides in the cremation ground. This is where the five elements are dissolved. This is the dissolving of attachment to the created world. It is in the heart of the devoted that this burning takes place and thus Kali dwells in our heart. Under Kali the devotee burns away all illusion and understands the gnosis he is given. The inner most flame is that of gnosis which Kali grants.

THE SEVEN MANIFESTATIONS OF KALI

What follows are the rituals and meditations for the seven manifestations of Kali. You may work with one manifestation per day with a day of rest between the next working.

MATANGI KALI

She is the violent reincarnation of the Goddess of Gnosis, Saraswati. She is the knowledge forbidden, that which the illusion fears. She lives at the edges of organized religion and watches. The green goddess is offered stale food by the left hand. She is often called Chandalini. She is usually worshipped in a temple and not in the home.

Ritual: The practitioner will draw the sigil of Matangi Kali on the ground in chalk carrying in his hands prayer beads. These beads should have 108 beads and at each bead the practitioner will chant "Matangi Kali, goddess of the forbidden knowledge. Green goddess I seek out your gnosis." This chanting is done while in your asana (meditation posture) and all your energy focus is on Matangi Kali.

The Seven Manifestations of Kali

Matangi Kali

Chhinna Masta

Shamsana Kali

Bagala Kali

Bhairavi Kali

Tara

Shodoshi

CHINNA MASTA

Chinna Masta means the beheaded. Here we see Kali holding her own severed head and drinking the blood from the stump at her own throat. At her feet are Kamdey and Devi engaging in sexual intercourse. This symbolizes death within creation.

Ritual: The practitioner will draw the sigil of Chhinna Kali on the ground in chalk. He will bring in a sacrificial animal. He will cut its throat and let the blood spill on the sigil.

"I shed blood and let prana flow. Let the energy of my spilt blood fill this chamber. As I empower you I ask that you empower me with true sight. Let me see beyond the veil, beyond causal abstraction and creation. Give me the true sight of what's to come. Grant me visions of whats to come, O wrathful and nurturing mother."

Shamsana Kali

She is the Goddess of the cremation grounds. Here is where creation will burn in the flames of the cosmic holocaust. She is often worshipped in or near a crematorium. This manifestation of Kali has no protruding tongue and has only two hands.

Meditation: Envision this manifestation and the cremation grounds where Kali resides. Smell the burning flesh, see the smoke and ash as you focus all your energy on this manifestation.

"Kali of the cremation grounds, dark mother of death, I ask that you burn the ego from my flesh and dissolve me back into the primordial darkness"
This meditation should go on for no less than one hour. Feel Kali strengthen your Azoth as you work toward liberation.

BAGALA KALI

A violent and abysmal manifestation of Kali this blood drenched form is irresistibly beautiful. She has a light complexion and pulls the tongue of those whom promote the creation.

Prayer: While focusing on the sigil repeat this prayer as many times as necessary. "Great mother of dark sorcery, mother of Gnosis. I see the beauty in your violence, see the splendor of your bloodshed. Cast a plague of violence upon this Earth, let the culling take place through aeonic sorcery.

Let the mundane butcher and batter each other. Bring forth the great cosmic holocaust, O mother of cosmic destruction."

BHAIRAVI KALI

She is the harbinger of death. Surrounding her are the spirits of the dead.

Meditation: You must acquire a human corpse for this meditation. You will get into your asana on top of the corpse and focus on the manifestation of Kali, chanting the words "Bhairavi Kali"

TARA

Light blue in color, she is a violent and sexual manifestation of Kali in which she is naked and clad in tiger skin.

Ritual: You are to carve this sigil on dark wood and carry it with you for a week. You are to look at the sigil once an hour for ten minutes during this week. When you sleep you will sleep with this sigil under your pillow. On the last day you will slice open your palm with an obsidian knife and bleed onto the sigil. Then you will meditate for one hour focusing on the bloody sigil.

Shodoshi

She is the seductress rising from the navel of Shiva. She is an adolescent.

No ritual or Meditation exists for this sigil. Some say it is a sigil of seduction and is given to the one you wish to be with in lust. It can be secretly placed at their place of residence under their bedroom window.

The Eight Manifestations of Bhairava

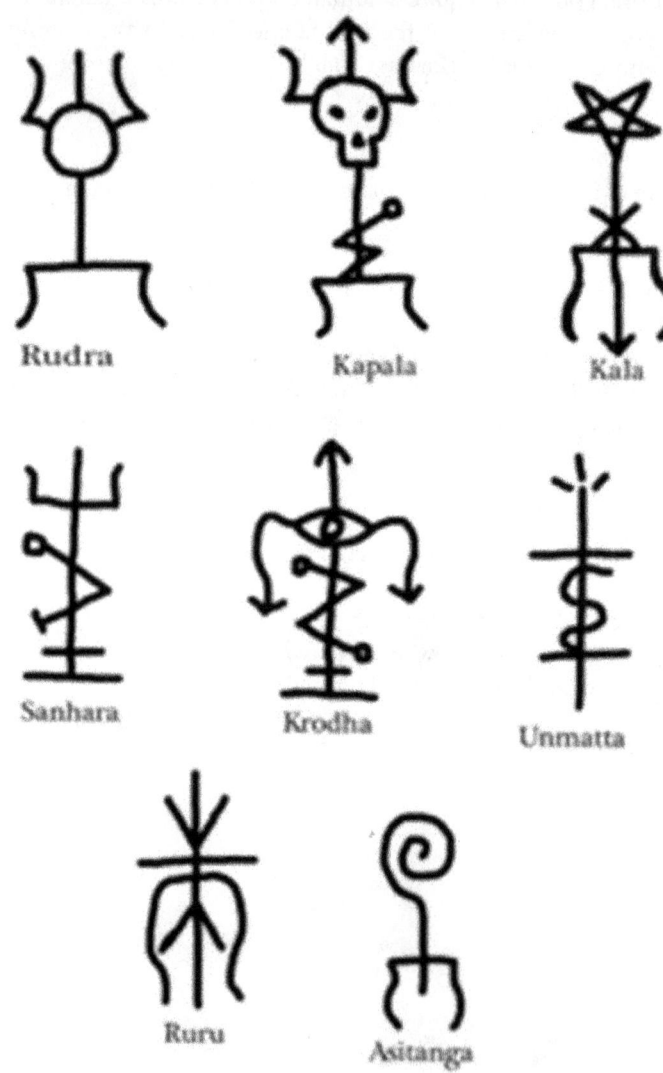

THE EIGHT MANIFESTATIONS OF BHAIRAVA

1. Through our suicide we awaken the spark. We are the children whom seek out Moksha, the great liberation and deconstruction of the wheel of Karma. Return us to the acausal womb, Lord Satan.

2. Bhairava, bring me forth the final holocaust. With your trident shovel the filth of humanity into the flames and use those flames to cremate all existence. He who carries the amputated head of Brahma. Let your black dog taste the blood.

3. Expose us to your dance, that of cosmic destruction. Spread storms of fire to burn all creation. Behold the eight manifestations

When meditating on the eight manifestations of Bhairava one may spend hours on a single manifestation. The meditation cannot be broken, and with this said one must be fully ready to take on this exhausting task. All chakras should be in balance before you even attempt this series of meditations. In the end one will find enlightenment and understanding.

First, find your Asana. Breath deep and let it out slowly. Now focus on the first manifestation which should be drawn on a dark wood with white chalk. Chant the manifestations name first loud and slow and lower the pitch as you speed it up until it is just a rapid movement of the lips.

Envision all the sigil has to offer. Focus on it and feel its power radiate throughout your body. Have it start as a dark light entering your feet and working its way up your body until finally exploding out the top of your skull. Do this until you are satisfied. A sensation, a power surge will be felt throughout your body to let you know that the meditation of that manifestation is complete. Then you are ready to move onto your next manifestation.

Once all manifestation meditations are complete you will observe all of the sigils at once chanting the name "Bhairava". This will be overwhelming for all manifestations will be flooding your mind and body at once and may be overwhelming. When you feel the final power surge than you know the meditation is complete.

You may now stand and exit the room. That night you will have a dream. Pay close attention to the dream and write in a journal everything you envisioned the next morning.

UNDERSTANDING THE LABYRINTH OF THE LILIN SOCIETY

What I call the Labyrinth is a means to test, jest, challenge and select new members. Truth be told, many members are selected upon merit but others with no prior dialogue with me go through the labyrinth. It's a trying and even humiliating path that will serve my own sadistic means, however, it also strengthens the initiate and teaches them to challenge themselves.

If an initiate tells me he failed a task I will ask why. If he admits he is weak then I see strength in him. If he tells me he is lazy I do not bother further. I got my test, my jest and I selected. These failures serve as entertainment for me and the rest of the Lilin Society.

Initiation has many levels. One must understand that to be serious at all times troubles the soul. We must have fun, at others expense. Many weak members squeak by but they are soon lost and consumed by the labyrinth, unable to differentiate fact from myth. They will spend their time praying to fictitious gods while the real members pray to the true ones.

Do you need to spend time doing physical labor to join, no, but what harm is there in challenging initiates and getting comic relief from their attempts. Initiates will all learn the secrets in time, some faster than others. Those who are familiar with the Order of the Nine Angles will understand sooner and cross through the Labyrinth.

I am a niner, a solo acting member of the Order of the Nine Angles. Does one need to follow the sevenfold way to be a member? That is a mundane thought frame don't you think? Anton Long stated himself that a Satanist follows no man. He is his own master. When Anton Long created his Labyrinth he did it for his own amusement.

To those who lived in the woods and committed fully at times to ridiculously laborious rituals to join I offer no apologies. It made you stronger and brought me cult amusement. Now the secret is out, well sort of. This is intended for the initiates whom I have selected into adeptship and took under my wing. Be proud to be the butt of my joke, be proud to put yourself through personal hell and challenge yourself, some of you for the first time in your life. I applaud you. Now although you won't see me hiking hours in the woods in just a robe in mid winter, I must say I respect those who have.

Now that the secret of the Labyrinth is out let's focus on the reason you joined the Lilin Society. To evolve.

THE PAIN OF EVOLUTION

So much has changed within the Lilin Society. From some of its teachings to its structure, but this is a part of evolution. If my writing was the same today as it was ten years ago then I have not evolved. Ten years ago I didn't believe in human sacrifice. Ten years ago I worked more in balance than with Chaos. Ten years ago I was Aka Paimon, today I am Asha'Shedim. This name change came with the change of my writing and beliefs. I have evolved.

Ten years from now I expect more changes for the Lilin Society. I expect more extreme and hard hitting views and teachings. I expect more extreme rituals and tests. I expect growth and maybe even more structure changes within the Lilin Society. This book contains the bulk of our current and up to date teachings. This book is vital for the member of the Lilin Society. The Lilin Society has brought me dramatic change and I know it can for its followers as well. The thing is, however, that it is earned and not given. The tried and tested path is a hard one to walk but the results last a lifetime.

When you evolve you will see the world differently. At first it's painful as depression and apathy takes hold of you. This is the dying ego struggling to hold on. Once you pass the abyss and see the beauty then you know you are there.

There is a misconception that a Satanist is misanthropic against everything in this created world. This is not so. Nature in itself is acausal. It is thriving with acausal energy and thus this is why the beauty can be soaked in. Many Satanists feel like they are posing as something they are not because they have attachments to this world, but the truth is that it is impossible to ever completely detach yourself from this world until you shed your Azoth free of all cosmic bondage. I still have my anchors despite my evolution.

We truly are gods among men for we have acknowledged the ability to change ourselves through spiritual alchemy. We can redesign ourselves to think different and acquire superhuman abilities once we tap into the acausal current.

I have been criticized for borrowing from the Order of Nine Angles. There are some strong similarities but there are differences as well. My beliefs are fused with Gnosticism and thus begins the deviation from traditional O9A beliefs. Their system works, plain and simple, so why not build off what works and evolve it further?

As the Lilin Society grows into the light, partly the result of the world wide web, our critics and enemies grow too. We will be scrutinized. Our Labyrinth of test, jest and select will be used against us to declare us as contradictory. But in the end the true believer will find their way. It is amazing the people I have met because of the Lilin Society.

One such "contradiction" that arose from an email to me was the fifteenth Satanic Point which reads "We are a society. We do not have priests or masters. The only real statue above member is the Council which serves to screen new members and enhance the Society and its direction. No Satanist shall bow before any other Satanists for it puts them in a position of submission. We do not submit."

The problem they have with it is that we have Masters and Mistresses within the Society. Well, let's look at this labyrinth of knowledge a little closer. Truth be told, this was written before I introduced the Master and Mistress into the Society, however, the final phrase still rings true. "No Satanist shall bow before any other Satanists for it puts them in a position of submission. We do not submit." We honor our Masters and Mistresses with respect for their knowledge and direction but we do not bow to them. We do not submit to any god, let alone man. The Master and Mistress was introduced in 2015 to mainly lead ceremonies and rituals.

Another of the Satanic Points that come to light as contradictory is the seventeenth point. "We believe in three forms of sorcery; Causal, Acausal and Aeonic." Later I state that we believe in Internal, External and Aeonic Sorcery. Even more confusing is that I describe in the Grimoire of Asha'Shedim that External Sorcery is Causal Sorcery, Internal Sorcery is Acausal Sorcery and Aeonic Sorcery is one that affects the masses. This is part of the Labyrinth to test and jest. Anyone familiar with the O9A knows that External Sorcery is that which affects the external world, Internal Sorcery is that that brings change from within while Aeonic Sorcery is the same as described earlier. I have had quite the laugh hearing people use the terms of this Satanic Point.

So why not change the Satanic Points to reflect what I explained here? Why should I disrupt the labyrinth of the Lilin Society? I will continue to allow it to run its course, and laugh at the hate mail from those whom have been misled due to their inferior ability to see beyond the large walls of the maze. So now we are in 2016. Expect a lot more tests in the future as I continue to evolve this thing I call the Lilin Society.

NO PRISONERS

What is peace? It is a means to continue existing in weakness and live a life in a meaningless manner. Many individuals, especially in modern times, avoid conflict at any cost. They cower at the thought that conflict may arise. These weak Jesus infused beings are a reflection of humanity in its current state. As true Satanists which have set out upon the sinister path we understand that evolution exists in conflict.

Some will call us radicals, extremists, but I ask what revolution has ever been won by anything described any less? War brings about the alchemy of the soul which burns the ego from the body. When faced with death then and only then can we truly cross the abyss.

Causal abstraction wants us to behave and remain weak. The enslavers of mankind control the minds of the peace seekers with sports, celebrities etc. They keep them content with fast food and an illusion of safety. We are here to remind them that the world is not safe. Acts of war and terrorism shock the very core of the peace seeker, dismantling their weak little lives.

War builds men and women to be hardened. War makes us predators whom seek out our prey. Through conquest man can change the world, not through peace. Man can conquer the world through war.

Our aeonic age of Homo Galaticus, our evolution, will come with war. We will fight and kill who we have to kill to win. We will do what needs to be done. The weak will be crushed and their bodies fed to Belphegor.

We must spread the sinister like a disease. We must support all wars and acts of terror, regardless if they are in sync with our sinister cause or not. We will use them to achieve our aeon and then crush them in the end.

How can we live if we have not faced death? I have faced death on more than one occasion, stared it in the face and saw its dark shadow. I grew from it, evolved.

We must be built of steel with a predator's eye. But I ask, how do we destroy the causal abstraction? We shall manipulate and infiltrate and once inside we shall burn it from within.

Some will call this a humanist agenda. Those individuals are ignorant to the path of evolution. Evolution is essential in order to break sephirotic bondage. How can we destroy creation when we can't even destroy causal abstraction?

These "occultists" live their lives in the mental and will never successfully cross the abyss unless they evolve. Evolution comes in conflict, pain and adversity. Aeonic sorcery exists in war, holocausts and terrorism.

We must infiltrate the sinister groups like Islamic terrorism much like we infiltrate causal abstraction. We must spread the terror of evolution by any means. Understand that this is a war and we take no prisoners.

I have stated before that violence is a dent in causal abstraction and that we must infiltrate instead. This is true, however, violence works. It is the core of evolution and must not be ignored.

We must become a nexion, a portal where the dark gods can channel acausal energy into this causal world. The nexion is a conduit of gnosis, the energy of our new aeon. We must allow the acausal spirits to possess us, to change us, to abolish all that we have been forced to learn and understand instead the truth. This will eat at our ego, an ego built and maintained by causal abstraction, and bind us to Azoth, our true self. This invocation of spirits begins the alchemy of the spirit and brings forth individual evolution. The acausal fuses with our own spirit and thus the pain and learning begins.

This is what separates the Lilin Society from many other Satanic groups. We are not mindless hedonistic beings, for over indulgence creates weakness. We understand that real change, true evolution is not only possible but inevitable to bring about the new aeon. It begins with killing the ego and freeing the Azoth.

BLOOD ORGY TO DARK MOTHER BAPHOMET

WARNING

The Following Ritual is intended for Adepts, Masters and Mistresses of the Lilin Society. Initiates should not partake. This ritual needs a Master and a Mistress

The Master or Mistress will begin the ceremony by invoking the elemental circle. This is as follows:

    Earth "Lirach tasa vefa wehlic, Belial"
    Air "Renich tasa uberaca biasa icar, Lucifer"
    Fire "Ganic tasa fubin, Flereous"
    Water "Jedan tasa hoet naca, Leviathan"

After this circle is consecrated. The Master walks around the circle. He is robed. Like all other participants this is the only article of clothing worn. If a member does not own a robe then they will be naked.

As the Master walks the circle the Adepts enter the room and line the perimeter of the circle. The Mistress reveals The Baphomet Art. The Baphomet Art is a painting or drawing of the true form of Baphomet. This is depicted as a beautiful mature woman who is nude. Her hands are stained with blood. She is holding the severed head of a Sacrificed priest. The priest has a beard. This art is placed upon the altar. Incense are lit as well as seven black candles.

The Master enters the circle and faces the altar. He screams. "Baphomet, bloody mother of Earth, bride of Satan. We call you, oh great and sexual shapeshifter."

Mistress (seductively): "Belial, great Earth element, we seek your assistance in calling the Mother of Earth, the Great Mother Baphomet to this chamber."
Master: "All chant"

The drummer now begins to beat the drum at a medium pace. The adepts chant "Ba-pho-met" loud over the drums. The room is full of energy as a virgin animal is brought into the room.

Mistress: "We shall attract you by shedding that energy you crave. This sacrifice is in your name Baphomet."

The Master uses an obsidian blade to kill the sacrifice, slitting its throat so that no energy is wasted and it dies without screaming. He collects the blood in a bowl. The Master and Mistress remove their robes and the Master raises the bowl above his head. He spills the blood over his naked body as the Mistress gets on her knees and crawls toward the Master.

The chanting and drumming gets faster. The Mistress performs fellatio upon the Master while she masturbates with her left finger. Right before the Master ejaculates he says the following phrase "Baphomet I ejaculate in your name."

The chanting and drumming stops as he ejaculates in the Mistresses mouth. The Mistress stands and walks over to the Baphomet Art. She spits the ejaculate onto the art and with her right hand paints blood on the hands of the woman in the painting.

Mistress: "Baphomet, I give you the gift of sacrifice, blood and semen. Fill this chamber with your spirit."

Now the adepts remove their robes and move into the center of the circle. While the Master and Mistress meditate in the center all around them an orgy takes place. The whole time they meditate on the image in the Art of Baphomet and focus all energy into her name. Each climax is energy given to the Blood Mother. The ritual is complete when the Master receives a sign from Baphomet. He then rises and says "Thank you Baphomet for joining us this evening. Now let you go in peace."

LESBIAN RITUAL OF THE DEMONIC FEMININE

WARNING
Only Grade Adept and above can partake in this ritual. It contains Lesbian acts which are expected to be performed by all participants.

This ritual must be conducted when the Mistress is on her menstrual cycle.

The Mistress enters the chamber naked. Following her are female adepts all wearing nothing except for a pentagram necklace. They follow her until they form a circle. The Mistress breaks from the circle and steps into the middle. The circle is established by the Mistress.

> Earth "Lirach tasa vefa wehlic, Belial"
> Air "Renich tasa uberaca biasa icar, Lucifer"
> Fire "Ganic tasa fubin, Flereous"
> Water "Jedan tasa hoet naca, Leviathan"

After this circle is consecrated.

Mistress: "Hear the demonic feminine names. Ardat Lili, great succubus, I call to thee. Batibat, nightmare demon, I call to you. Empusa, great shapeshifter, I call you. Gorgon, bringer of death, I call to you. Hantu Kopek, nightmare demon, I call to you. Lamashtu, seven witches in one, I call to you. Lamia, vampire, I call to you. Lilith, great anti cosmic mother, I call to you. Naahma, great succubus, I call to you. Palden Lhamo, guardian, I call to you. Yuki-Onna, blood drinker, I call to you. Great and powerful Blood Mother Baphomet, I call to you. I call to the demonic feminine to come to this chamber and strengthen our feminine powers. By the Yoni and red tincture, by the womb and the life giving organs, by the feminine seduction we call ye all forth."

Boneset herbs are now burnt as the adepts all begin chanting "Ba-pho-met". They are on their knees and turn their heads counter clockwise with each chanting of the name. The Mistress goes into a trance and allows the energies of the demonic feminine to enter her body. She then stands over a bowl and squats over it, allowing the blood of her menstrual cycle to spill into the bowl. She then stands and holds a chalice of water.

Mistress: "Leviathan, bless this wine"

She then mixes the wine with the blood. Sprinkled in it ground dandelions, chamomile flowers and damiana leaves. The mixture is then raised above her head.

Mistress: "Behold the elixir of our feminine powers. Bless this bowl oh great demonic feminine."

The Mistress takes a sip and then passes it to an adept. Each adept takes a sip and then kisses the Mistress. When this is complete the adepts all lay down on the ground. The Mistress then walks around the circle placing her vagina in the eager mouths of the adepts one at a time for five minutes at a time. The adepts should lick the vagina and anus as well during this. When the circle is complete the adepts will engage in a lesbian orgy while the Mistress meditates and masturbates.

The Mistress will focus all the sexual energy in the room. She will envision it entering her body and empowering her. She will accept the powers of the demonic feminine. When she climaxes the orgy ends and the adepts all stand back in the circle.

The Mistress walks around the circle. She puts her fingers into her vagina and removes some blood. She then makes a small mark on the forehead of the adept, one at a time. Once all adepts have been marked the Mistress returns to the center of the circle.

Mistress: "This concludes our ritual. All demons of the demonic feminine may return to the acausal world. Thank you for your presence this evening."

Now the Mistress leaves as the line of adepts follow. After this all participants will take a bath in Queen Elizabeth Root.

THE LILIN SOCIETY'S BLACK MASS

Participants:
Master: Dressed in purple
Mistress of Earth: Dressed in scarlet robes
Altar Adept: Nude female who lays on the altar
Priest: Dressed in white
Congregation: Adepts and Initiates in black

This ritual is performed either indoors or in a cave. Hazel incense are burnt. There are several chalices full of strong wine. There are plenty of black candles lit. Several plates with the consecrated cakes. These are baked the night before by the Mistress and blessed, dedicated to Satan. The cakes consist of honey, spring water, sea salt, wheat flour, eggs and animal fat. One plate is set aside for the ritual hosts.

The mass begins when the Master claps his hands. The Mistress of Earth turns to the congregation, uses her hands to make the sign of the inverted pentegram.

Mistress of Earth: "I descend down to the altar of Hell"

Priest: "To Satan, the giver of life"

All: "Our father, of Cosmic Chaos, hallowed be thy name. Shall the bridge to the other side be built, to give us the gift of Gnosis, to deliver us to evil as well as temptation, for we stand at the temple of pleasure."

Master: "May Satan, the ruler of Sitra Achra, grant us our desires.

All: "Lord Satan hear us, hear us. I follow the god of Cosmic Chaos, and that is Satan. He who will reign over Earth through aeonic sorcery. I believe in one temple, and that is the temple of the Lilin Society. Word which triumphs over all, the word of ecstasy. And I believe in the law of the aeon, and this aeon is marked with sacrifice, the spilling of blood for which I shed no tears since I gave praise to Lord Satan, the giver of the Black Flame. I look forward to his reign and the pleasures to come.

The Mistress of the Earth kisses the Master, then she turns to the congregation.

Mistress of the Earth: "May Satan be with you."

Master: "Veni, omnipotens asternae diablos

Mistress of the Earth: "By the word of Lord Satan, I give praise to you."

The Mistress of the Earth now kisses the priest.

Mistress of the Earth: "My Lord, bringer of enlightenment. I greet you who cause us to struggle and seek out forbidden knowledge, that which was denied to us in the Garden of Eden."

The Master now begins to chant "Chav-a-joth"

Mistress of the Earth: "Blessed are the strong for they shall inherit the Earth."

She kisses the chest of the priest.

Mistress of the Earth: "Blessed are the proud for they shall breed gods."

She kisses the penis of the priest.

Mistress of the Earth: "Let the humble and the meek die in their misery.

She kisses the Master and then walks over to the congregation and kisses each member on the lips. After this the priest hands the plate to the Mistress of the Earth. The Mistress of the Earth holds the plate above the nude body of the altar adept.

Mistress of the Earth: "Praised are you, my Lord and lover. Between my legs are moist in wanting you. Through our evil we have the dirt, by our boldness and strength, it will become for us a joy in this life.

All: "All Hail Satan, Lord of Death"

The Mistress of the Earth places the plate on the belly of the Altar Adept and quietly speaks.

Mistress of the Earth: "Suscipe, Satanas, munus quad tibi offerimus memoriam Recolentes vindex

The priest quietly repeats "Sanctissimi Corporis Satanas"

The priest begins to masturbate the Altar Adept. When the Altar Adept climaxes the plate is removed from the belly of the Altar Adept and handed to the Mistress of the Earth. She holds it high.

Mistress of the Earth: "May the gifts of Satan forever be with you."

All: "As they are with you."

The Mistress of Earth returns the plate to the belly of the Altar Adept and then grabs a chalice, holding it high.

Mistress of the Earth: "Praised are you, my Lord, by the defiant. Through our arrogance and pride we have this drink. Let this be the elixir that lifts the veil the Demiurge has placed upon us.

She sprinkles wine onto the body of the Altar Adept, then towards the congregation. She then returns the chalice to the altar.

Mistress of Earth: "With pride in my heart I give praise to those who drove the nails and he who thrust the spear into the body of the pathetic Christ, the imposter. May his followers rot in their rejection and filth."

Master: "Do you renounce Jesus Christ and all his teachings and work?"

All: "We do renounce Jesus Christ, the great deceiver and his works."

Master: "Do you affirm Satan?"

All: "We do affirm Satan."

The Master begins to chant "Sit-ra-ah-ra" while the Mistress of the Earth retrieves the plate.

Mistress of the Earth: "I who am the joys and pleasure of life which strong men have forever sought, am come to show you my body and my blood."

The Mistress hands the plate to the priest and removes her robe. She runs her hands up and down her naked body while speaking.

Mistress of the Earth: "Remember all of you gathered here that nothing is as beautiful except man, but most beautiful is woman."

The priest brings the cakes and wine to the congregation. When all finish eating and drinking the Mistress of Earth holds the empty plate high.

Mistress of the Earth: "Behold, the dirt of the earth which the humble will eat."

The Mistress of the Earth now begins to fling cakes at the congregation from another plate which the congregation tramples beneath their feet. The Mistress of the Earth claps three times.

Mistress of the Earth: "Dance, I command you."

The congregation begins to dance counter clockwise chanting "Satan" as they dance. The Mistress of the Earth catches them one by one and kisses them, running their hands over her naked body. After the kiss the congregation member's robe is removed and when all are naked the Mistress of the Earth stands in the center of the dancing members with her arms uplifted.

Mistress of the Earth: "Let the Churches of the imposter and impotent Lord, Jesus Christ, burn in Satanic wrath. Let the weak scum who worship the dog called Christ suffer a miserable death. Let chaos reign. Let there be sacrifice."

She signals for the priest who stops the dancer of his choice. The congregation then indulges in an orgy. The Mistress helps down the Altar Adept who joins the orgy. The energies of this ritual are directed towards a specific intention.

Thus ends the Black Mass of the Lilin Society.

THE NECROSEXUAL RITES OF THE WHORE LILITH

This is a sexual rite ritual to Lilith. This is an intense ritual which blends necromancy with sexual sorcery. This ritual is meant for a coven. This ceremony involves role play. Only the rank of Adept and above may partake.

Participants:

Lilith: This role is played by the Mistress.
Adam: This role is played by an Adept
Samael: This role is played by the Master
The Voice: This role is played by an adept and speaks during the ceremony.
Senoy, Sansenoy and Semangelof: Three angels played by three adepts
Singer: Female adept.

Congregation: Made up of Adepts.

The coven will enter an old crypt at night on a Tuesday during the hour of Mars. Once inside light many red and black candles and set up an altar. At this altar place herbs, wands, and human bones. Several mirrors are placed around the crypt.

Open one of the caskets to get a dead body. If the crypt is too secure you can exhume a dead body from a nearby grave. To avoid the legal ramifications that may arise from grave robbing one may substitute legally acquired human bones. If bones are used a total of ten must be used.

Black berries and dill are placed all around the outside of the crypt for protection from others stumbling upon the ritual. On the inside of the crypt ginger is sprinkled in all corners. All men will wear a musky cologne or oil and all women will wear a black licorice scent. Cinnamon should be burned as an incense alongside cedarwood.

Each member will now use red paint and draw the sigil of Lilith on their bellies. (Note: You don't need to put the words LILITH in the circle.)

Start by declaring a circle. The Master does this.

>   Earth "Lirach tasa vefa wehlic, Belial"
>   Air "Renich tasa uberaca biasa icar, Lucifer"
>   Fire "Ganic tasa fubin, Flereous"
>   Water "Jedan tasa hoet naca, Leviathan"

After the circle is declared the participants now will go into their roles.

Voice: We call deep into the acausal world and call out to Lilith. We perform this ritual in your honor. Tonight we will tell the story of Lilith and Adam in the Garden of Eden. At first Adam was created and he was lonely. He asked the creator to make him a companion. The creator listened and obeyed. He made a woman from the Earth but this time he used filth rather than pure dust. Her name was Lilith.

Now Adam and Lilith step out as the congregation watches. Congregation: All hail Lilith

Lilith starts kissing Adam and running her hands over his genitalia. He does the same to her. They lay on the ground and Lilith climbs on top.

Voice: That night when they were about to engage in intercourse Adam told Lilith that she had to be on the bottom for that is where women belong, below men. Lilith responded that they were both made from the Earth therefore they were equals. Adam said she was made from filth and there for she must submit to superiority.

Lilith immediately stands up and turns away.

Voice: And this upset Lilith for she knew the power of her femininity and was insulted by Adam's belittling her. She knew her natural sorcery skills and how they tied in with her femininity. So she rose into the air and the wind took her away.

Adam puts his head in his hands and pretends to cry. He gets up and leaves the altar area. Samael enters from stage right and immediately there is an attraction between Lilith and himself.

Voice: Lilith met the great Samael Congregation: Hail Samael Voice: The two engaged in sex by the Red sea.

With Lilith on top Samael and Lilith begin to engage in sex. Voice: The two had children, half demons called Lilin. Congregation: Hail the Lilin

Voice: She had more than one hundred per day. Adam cried to the creator and begged him to return his wife to him. The creator sent three angels, Senoy, Sansenoy and Semangelof, to the Red Sea to retrieve Lilith.

The three angels enter stage left. They stumble upon Lilith and Samael engaged in intercourse.

Angel: Return to Adam or we will drown you.

Lilith continues to have sex but responds.

Lilith: How can I return to Adam as an honest housewife after my stay at the Red Sea.

Angel: Return or we will kill you.

Lilith: You can't kill me, God has ordered me to take charge of all newborn children: boys up to the eighth day of life, that of circumcision; girls up to the twentieth day. I vow to kill the children of Adam however, if you leave now I promise that if I ever see your three names or likenesses displayed in an amulet above a newborn child, I promise to spare it.

Voice: The angels agreed and returned to the creator with the news. The creator was furious and ordered that one hundred of Lilith's children be killed each day. Lilith ruled as queen in Zmargad, and again in Sheba; and was the demoness who destroyed Job's sons. Yet she escaped the curse of death which overtook Adam, since they had parted long before the Fall. Lilith and her sister Naamah not only strangled sleeping infants but also seduced dreaming men, any one of whom, sleeping alone, may become their victim. They became terrors of the night, succubi, the great whores.

Congregation: Hail the whores.

Voice: And so is the story of the Queen of Demons. She is the mother of crib death, mother of abortions. Her strong sexuality is linked with death. So tonight we will also link death with sexuality.

Two adepts now bring out the corpse. Lilith and Samael stand before it.

The Voice uses the wand to draw the sigil of Lilith in the sky.

Voice: Lilith we honor you today as we strengthen the bond between sex and death.

Samael and Lilith engage in sexual intercourse while laying on top of the corpse. Immediately the whole congregation breaks out in orgy except for the Voice. He chants "Lillith" while continuously drawing her sigil in the sky above those engaged in sex.

During the orgy women should be on top. They will play the dominant role. Lilith should, during the act, masturbate herself with human bones.

Voice: Great and powerful Lilith, witness your children engaged in sexual abominations. We do this in your honor. We do this to honor your name. Great whore of Sitra Achra, we praise you. Every mirror is a gateway to the Other Side, to Sitra Achra. It is a window peering deep into the cave of Lilith. Lilith makes her home in every mirror. Lilith, show us the shadow of the moon."

The singer, while engaging in sex, begins to sing the following.

Singer: I invoke you, mother of the darkness! I invoke you, mother of the night! I shall make a golden cradle to make a place for gnosis. I shall awaken the black flame to warm gnosis inside. I shall put my hands in your lap for you to bless and use. I shall put my heart in your lap to be caressed by your blessing hands. Lilith, Lady of the evening star, Inanna, Lilith of the morning star, Lilith, lady of the dark moon. I call to you, I call to you.

After this song the coven will rise and exit the crypt. They will dance nude in the moon light singing the following song.

Great Lilith, dark mother of desire Great Lilith, I surrender to your lust Great Lilith, may you guide me with strength Great Lilith, Great Lilith.

After singing the song several times the coven will leave. Each member will wait until the dark moon (three days leading up to the new moon) and perform the following ritual alone.

First light some candles around your bathtub. Light some cinnamon incense and place the following herbs into the bath water: sage, chamomile, cinnamon, lemon balm, sandalwood, lavender, rosemary, hyssop, sweetgrass and peppermint.

Breathe deeply, taking in the scents of the herbal oils in the water.

After you complete your cleansing purification bath you will prepare yourself a mug of hot, soothing herbal tea of lavender, peppermint and rosemary. Drink your tea as you set up your space.

CREATING SACRED SPACE:

Set up a small altar with a single red candle, lotus incense and image of Lilith. Purify the space and yourself with sage. Cast a circle in the following manner.

> Earth "Lirach tasa vefa wehlic, Belial"
> Air "Renich tasa uberaca biasa icar, Lucifer"
> Fire "Ganic tasa fubin, Flereous"
> Water "Jedan tasa hoet naca, Leviathan"

Preparation:

Take your athame and cut your left finger. Spill a couple drops of blood and mix with red ink. Draw the following hebrew characters: The name of Lilith

לילית on the palm of your left hand and the name of Samael סמאל on the palm of your right hand.

Pour red wine into the chalice and put it on the altar. Light your incense and red candle. Dim or darken the lights so that your small candle sheds light on the symbolic item on the altar. Finish your tea. Sit comfortably and set your gaze on your altar. When you are ready, begin the ritual.

Invocation:

"Tonight, on this darkest of nights, I am prepared to journey into the darkness. I gaze deep into the abyss and into Sitra Achra where I see my queen. I call to you, Lilith.

Lilith, ancient one, I invoke you to guide me into the darkness of Sitra Achra. Enter my flesh temple and allow me to see and understand."

Drink from the chalice. Now meditate on the image of Lilith. Let her come to you. She may leave images in your mind, symbols or words. When you are finished write them down in your journal with the red ink.

Now you will masturbate to her image. At the moment of climax say her name. When you are done thank Lilith and blow out the candle.

SODOMY: A BLASPHEMY FROM THE DEVIL

A Guide for Heterosexual, Lesbian and Homosexual Sodomy Sorcery

She was bent over and I spread her butt cheeks to gaze into her beautiful asshole, and without any condom, I pushed my dripping rampant cock straight up her ass. She gasped, threw her head back and started pulling her own nipples.

He rose quickly and I pushed him against the wall and rubbed my huge, hard cock between his ass cheeks. He moaned and whimpered and I wrapped one hand around his mouth as I probed his asshole with my head.

We made out with each other's asses for what must've been a half hour before Lucy produced a dildo and slid it up my fat ass. She knew from my recent exploits with her ex- boyfriend that I loved it up the ass. She buttfucked me thoroughly with the dildo, still in the 69 position, licking and smacking on my cunt as she fucked my ass. At that point I really was screaming; no guy's cock had ever felt so goddamned good rammed up my bottom.

The three little paragraphs, although one a heterosexual, one a homosexual and one a lesbian experience they all have the same thing in common; anal sex or sodomy.

What is it about sodomy that drives people to try it? Is it the taboo to engage in something not natural, something beyond the grace of the creator? Is it out of sheer blasphemy? Is it the excitement of defying the church and engaging in acts that make the creator shudder? Or does it just feel so damn good in the ass?

I am a heterosexual male and I have stuck my penis between quite a few females butt cheeks in my time. I often ask them afterwards if they enjoyed it. Usually they are dazed, barely able to speak, but they manage to let out the word "yes."

One woman described it to me as the perfect combination of pleasure and pain. Isn't that a perfect metaphor for life on this planet? Life is like anal sex? Whereas vaginal intercourse is strictly pleasure with a "natural" means of reproducing, anal intercourse is hardly anything but "natural". You can't get pregnant from it and there is of course the pain.

Why is it that we like pain so much?

The Jews, as sexually void of pleasure as they once were, would blame the anal sex epidemic on Yezer Ha-Ra. These evil inclinations are an embodiment of that within our heart and minds that tempts us to do what we know is wrong. The Jews believe it is a part of human nature in all men and women that at all times acts as an adversary to good, natural and "holy". The Yezer Ha-Ra is an irresistible, lustful urge to make us do what is "unnatural", like anal intercourse.

The church is against it, mundanes usually hate it so in short all us anal intercourse loving sexual deviants over come by our Yezer Ha-Ra are the all powerful sodomy sorcerers of blasphemy.

What would happen if the entire world, through aeonic sorcery, gave up vaginal intercourse and traded it for the pleasures and pains of sodomy? Well, for starters the human race would die off and the Creator would have no more slaves to serve him and worship him. Blasphemy would be law meaning all causal abstractions would no longer have a religious backbone and thus weaken. Men and women would no longer feel just the pleasures of life but the pains of it too, and they would begin to understand, understand the absolute power of sodomy.

Anal sex, whether heterosexual, homosexual or lesbian in nature has always been the sex of the Devil. When it comes to sodomy one cannot ignore the powerful sorcery of the act. To have the cavity between your cheeks violated with a phallus, real or fake, will bring your sorcery to new levels.

If you're a straight male show that woman the power of your phallus. If you're a lesbian use that strap on dildo and make her love your cock. If you're a gay male slam that prostate. Take turns switching off from giving and receiving to feel the full experience for the homosexual is the master of sodomy sorcery.

WORSHIP SATAN AND ENGAGE IN ANAL SEX.

Sodomy Ritual (heterosexual)

The man will use body paint and on the left cheek of his partner he will draw the sigil of Satan, and on the right cheek he will draw the sigil of Lilith. On her lower back he will paint a pentagram.

Let cinnamon burn during this ritual. If music is played make sure it's violent and full of minor notes. Have red candles lit all around the altar (in this case a bed can be an altar) and turn off all artificial lighting.

The man will paint the sigil of Lucifer upon his chest. He will not wear a condom. He will use as little lubricant as necessary, just enough to get his penis inside her anus.

Man: In the name of Satan, ruler of Sitra Achra, I perform this blasphemous sexual rite in your honor. Let each thrust be felt by the Creator. May each thrust shake his kingdom and may each thrust kill an angel."

The man then slides his penis into her ass. During the act it would add to the blasphemy to engage in other violent sexual acts such as pulling hair, slapping of the buttocks, scratching, cutting, biting etc.

The woman must clear her mind as must the man. She must focus on the flames of hell as she feels his phallus scrape her insides. She must focus on the pain just as much as the pleasure and envision the lustful union of Satan and Lilith. She must take the role of Lilith, and he must take the role of Satan. She is not submitting, she wants this. She must be vocal about her wants.

Woman: In the name of Satan fuck my ass harder. Make me feel the agony. Hurt me, I demand it.

She must envision the filthy lust of the sex demons dropping down from the sky. She must chant "fuck my ass" in rhythm with each thrust. The female during this ritual is the real sorcerer.

When the man is about to ejaculate he will pull out of her ass and masturbate himself. When he ejaculates he will scream "Hail Satan" and ejaculate onto the pentagram on her back.

When the ritual is complete the woman will meditate for an undetermined amount of time, focusing on the pain and pleasure and direct all energy to what she desires.

SODOMY RITUAL (LESBIAN)

The lesbian ritual is exactly the same however there is no ejaculation. A strap on dildo is better than a regular one. This is the least effective of the three rituals.

SODOMY RITUAL (HOMOSEXUAL)

Now you homosexuals really will have an advantage over the heterosexuals or the lesbians. This is where the real powerful sorcery comes into play. The homosexuals will engage in the same exact ritual as the heterosexual ritual but after the "giver" ejaculates onto the "receiver", instead of meditation, the ritual continues while the two switch roles and go through the ritual again in which the "giver" becomes the "receiver" and the "receiver" the "giver". To add more power to the ritual after the "giver" ejaculates onto the pentagram he can bend down and lick the semen off the "receiver's" back.

ADDITIONAL BLASPHEMOUS SEX ACTS

Other acts to try during these three rituals is analingus (anus licking), anal stimulation with fingers, fisting of the anus and if more than two people are present during the heterosexual or lesbian ritual, double penetration.

Try everything goes orgies, rape play, bondage and S&M, forced gay (straight playing gay for sake of ritual), asphyxiation, blasphemous role play (Judas penetrating Jesus), mummification (not literally). If you have a strong stomach try urination, scat (feces).

Be a sexual sorcerer, the more deviant the better the outcome will be.

SEXUALITY IN THE LILIN SOCIETY

As humans bound to the causal world we tend to be hedonistic. We don't want to be here but since we are here we make the best of it. One of the strongest indulgences we can practice is that of sex. Sex has qualities in sorcery. Take the fact that the Christians all shun sex. Carnal displays like pornography are blasphemous and thus act as a form of aeonic sorcery.

But going deeper into sexuality and sorcery one must understand the extreme amount of energy and concentration that goes into the act. The practitioner is focused as he or she strives to reach their climax. When that climax is released the energy is massive. To harvest this energy and use it in ritual ceremony is important. I encourage all to use sex in their art.

Now the debate has come up about homosexuality. I don't understand why this would be something the Lilin Society wouldn't embrace. Homosexual and Lesbian acts are a spit in the face of the cosmic creator as well as his little demiurgic cults. Same sex relations are aeonic sorcery on their own accord as is group sex, bisexuality and so on. That goes for sexual acts as well such as cunnilingus, analingus, sodomy, oral and so on.

Now understand that I'm not saying that if it isn't in your nature to indulge in homosexual acts then you should do it for the sake of aeonic sorcery. I am just explaining why the Lilin Society allows homosexual, lesbian, bisexual, transgendered and so on to join. Indulge in the most sacred energy force you have.

GUIDE TO SEXUAL SORCERY

The first step in performing sexual sorcery is finding a suitable partner. The operator must feel empathy in their partner and their partner must have a genuine interest in sorcery, understand the art and desire a successful outcome. One should really seek out a perfect partner whom has all these qualities and not just settle on anyone.

The purpose of sexual workings is to use sexual energy which is generated by the act of intercourse. The sexual act must be done with planet governing the desire. When the planet is rising at the place where the act is taking place then this is constructive work. If the planet is setting then you are working in destruction.

The whole thing should be ritualized. Use incense and candles used with the planet. Choose a place naturally magical, someplace full of aura. You may use your chamber for such acts. There should be an altar complete with candles. It also helps if both partners bathe each other in an herbal bath using herbs to enhance their working.

The desire of the working should be clear. Visualization during the act is important. One might even suggest ingesting psychedelic drugs, the venom of Samael.

When working in heterosexual workings the male arouses the female by running his hand up and down her spine and shoulders. He then will arouse her through the act of oral sex. At the beginning of the act the female will visualize the desire chosen. The female will chant the desire rhythmically with the thrusts of her partner until climax.

The female is the gate through which the acausal energy will flow making her role ever so important. She should envision this acausal energy flowing throughout her body as a warm erotic light coming from the sky.

After the act the two will meditate for a period of time before announcing that the ritual is complete.

In Sapphic workings involves two females. This is a very powerful sorcery. Both partners combine their visualization and chanting during the act of cunnilingus. Uranian workings involves two men. They will stimulate each other orally at first and then engage in sodomy. The one being penetrated will play the role of the feminine naturally and will be in control of visualization and chanting.

Bisexual acts are very powerful. If it involves a man and two women one woman is penetrated while that woman orally stimulates the other woman. Both women are chanting. In acts involving a woman and two men one man will penetrate the woman and then be penetrated by the other man. This man both giving and receiving has a powerful role in the outcome of the act for he is visualizing and chanting while he is engaging the female who is also visualizing and chanting.

Group sex is the final form of sexual magic. This is a very powerful method especially if bisexuality is involved. One must realize that the sexual act is a means of achieving a goal in sorcery and not pleasuring themselves. They should shed all homophobic fears if engaging in bisexual workings and understand it's just a step in the art.

EVIL

Satan is evil and the Satanist personifies the Lord of Evil. There is no sugar coating this. If we behave in society it is simply to avoid the ramifications of our actions. In the end the so called laws are subjective and thus are null. The causal world is an illusion, as is Karma. We are forced in this state to obey by these "rules" simply because of our imprisonment within the Cosmic Order.

Now let us back up for a second by allowing me to say that there is no good nor is there evil. This seems like I just contradicted myself but I assure you that I haven't. One must remember that this world is an illusion, a lie, and the concept of good and evil is a means to keep human cattle in check.

The masses are swept up into the hysteria of good and evil and thus we personify the evil. This is us making a stance as the adversary. What is good I ask? The answer is a slave mentality, slave morality, ignorance of the truth, a weak spirit with a strong ego, passive, masochistic in nature, apathetic, inability to think for oneself, obeying laws without question, overall weakness and a total submission to the demiurge. If this is good then the Satanist is truly evil.

Temples and Churches like the Temple of Set swear allegiance to the dark Lord yet they try to portray Satan as a loving, nurturing and family friendly character with moral ethics. They can try all they want but the truth is not to be ignored. Satan is abysmal, wrathful and as we personify his will we are the misanthropes of society and the evil doers.

We do not seek out public approval, such as the Temple of Set, for we are not weak minded. We also believe in committing acts of evil in order to create aeonic sorcery, a sorcery which feeds on emotion and spreads like a wild fire. Aeonic Satanic Sorcery is a weapon in the war between the causal and the acausal.

LIBER INFERNO 2016

ONE.

To understand the truth is to understand the infinite. It is to understand the primordial darkness of Tiamat's womb. Splendid are her abortions.

I speak through this man, and this wisdom descends from the land of shells.

He who forsakes the ego, that which makes him mortal, becomes a personification of those whom live in the land of shells.

Those whom swear allegiances with chaos are not betrayers, unlike those whom surrendered freedom for the chains of the Tetragrammaton, the dreaded demiurge.

11 is a magical number. In this number many secrets hide. Discover the Chavajoth.

Understand that squares exist, and squares help you discover.

You must find squares and study squares.

Add, multiply, and understand. Gematria is the language of the acausal.

Mathematics is the language universal.

What is a number? It is a symbol. Symbols are a language.

But do not forget that your reality is not reality for truth does not exist within the egg, but rather outside in the timeless, eternal, pan dimensional chaos. Ah, o return me to Sitra Achra, o dark mother of desire!

Arachnid mother. In death there is rebirth. Energy is eternal. We are energy and we cannot be created nor destroyed.

We cannot be created but our flesh prison can.

And since it cannot be created just recycled, where, o mortals bewildered, do you think such energy came from? Where has it been imported from when the cosmic order was built, ruled by the dreaded demiurge!

Hail Lucifer, bearer of light!

Illuminate my path and show me to the cleansing fires of Moloch! Shower me with the flames that burn the ego from the spirit.

Show me the flames to toss the children. I shall obey.

Show me the flames within, and help teach me with the squares.

Moloch, it is you we dedicate much blood, and we shall feed.

Witness the absolute beauty, the fetus hanging from the umbilical cord. There is birth in death, and death is not an end. Understand that living lives according to subjective morality will not bring you rebirth in a paradise. Forsake these pipe dreams, propaganda and lies from the demiurge.

Do what thou wilt, shall be the whole of the law. Understand this law, and live by this law.

Find your path to true will.

Find Ahriman!

TWO

From the womb Ahriman tore his way out, and with a kiss he gave woman the menstrual cycle!

Praise be to Ahriman!

O he who created the dragon whom built planets in an act of opposition!

Az

Seducer and adversary. Unite the 5 and the 6 and give us 11

This is man's Divine Will!

And what will is that?

Do what thou wilt, shall be the whole of the law!

What is dead is alive what is alive is dead!

Murder is murder so why deny man his murderous instinct. Let a wolf feed.

I say let him have it.

There is no right, there is no wrong

There is only here and now!

ALL HAIL AHRIMAN, ALL HAIL THE GIFT OF AHRIMAN

ALL HAIL THE BLACK FLAME

HAIL AHRIMAN!

THREE

SMASH THE TETRAGRAMMATON

Churches of cosmic order exist all around us in many forms in many names.

BURN THEM ALL TO THE GROUND

DESTROY CAUSAL ABSTRACTION WHICH ENSLAVES US HERE AND NOW!

Let the dirt inherit their ashes; let their sheep die by satanic wrath!

LET THE WORLD BURN IN THE BLACK FLAME!

Heed these words!

Do not disregard, for to disregard is to be ignorant and to be ignorant is to be mindless and to be mindless is to be mortal. Little ignorant mortals floating in a placid sea of cosmic yolk! Are ye ready to understand the use of your spine?

Feel the electricity in the pineal gland!

Feel me, hear me and understand me for I am he!

Knowledge has been planted in the brain of this man! And burn the world, this world as was envisioned by the demiurge!

Let chaos fuel the fires! Let the bodies pile high and set them ablaze. Among the cooked meat and melting flesh I find contentment.

Burn this world in the flame of Moloch

This shall be the time of cleansing and the time of cleansing shall remain secret until mankind is ready to understand what is necessary. Nude forms dance wildly in the ashes of those dying, as smoke bellows and spills over the sky from chimneys. Feed the flames of Moloch with the bodies. Let the Cosmic Holocaust begin!

And when they ask tell them not

For our followers will be the shadows, for in the shadows we seek comfort, and in the shadows we will fight for we are the night predators!

He who flees the light

FOUR

I looked to the sky and saw nothing. I looked under the dirt, and I found nothing. When I closed my eyes and forgot the world around me, I found the seed.

O, the seed is small and black. It is the serpent's seed, the seed of Apep. This seed is planted in my brain and I shall take great care of it now that I have discovered it.

I opened my eyes, and I return to the world as is envisioned by Tetragrammaton. I am aware of the restraints of this cosmic order. When I close my eyes I am free of the Demiurge and am left to water the seed, the gift of Ahriman, and the seed of Apep.

Ah, and from a large goblet do I water this seed. With the slain blood of our father, of Kingu, whom sat at the throne of Chaos with Tiamat, and whom was struck down by Marduk, and forget not, oh Children of Samael-Lilith, that the same blood pumps in your veins.

We inhabit bodies of clay. Our spirit, the eternal spark, the imported energy, it is imprisoned in clay. But how did you fire that clay prison? The burning black flame of Ahriman!

O, beings born of fireless smoke, o beings of demonic orders, we join you in misanthropy!

Blinded are thee, o creatures of habit, and thou habits have weakened thee, o dogs of Christ. Under Satanic might your unstable empire, your Causal Abstractions, will be demolished as we flex. From the fallen kingdom, from the ashes of your churches, a new empire will rise, an empire led through the night by the bearer of light. This is our dawn!

And let the meek rot, let their corpses be fed to their dogs, for we must show no pity for those whom are already dead. Death is a gift to slaves.

Take this here, take this now, and let this be the day of heaven and hell. Pull free the veil, and break the chains that bind. Be blinded not by the illusionary light of the dreaded Demiurge, understand the limitations of our universe, and understand the powers of the consciousness, the powers of the mind. Life is here and now, so be here and now, but understand that what is here and now is no more once the body, heart and brain rot. When the blood ceases, our consciousness is eternal, for energy cannot be created nor destroyed, so therefore only death is eternal. Death is an illusion, life is a dream.

Understand that only in death will you be free, so welcome death.

Shed your anchors to prevent the vicious cycle of rebirth.

Lucifer, is the father of Dissidence, and dissidence is the father of Satanism. With pens and steel, our message will be felt. With ink and blood, our oaths shall be read. With a thundering battle cry, which deafens the ears of the sheep, will my voice be heard.

I AM THE WOLF AMONG THE FLOCK!

But I concern myself not with the sheep. Feeble minds are feeble until the end, but the Shepherd whom bewilders millions and mildews minds shall be my target. He, the bastard son, feel the hilt of my sword enter your disgusting, rancid heart. And when I strike down the pathetic son, your impotent mad redeemer, then my Luciferian hordes, the Wrathful Gods, the Chavajoth, shall storm the ivory gates and drink the blood from the severed neck of your rotting Jehovah.

Hail the first murderer and first Satanist, Qayin, and his beautiful sister, Luluwa.

FIVE

Worship me, for I am the serpent which brought you to the tree. Ignorant you would be without me, and a slave to the demiurge, blinded by illusionary light. I am the way, be bewildered not, follow not the flock for my path will lead to all that is all and all that is just.

Treat he not different from she. Treat not this from that or that from this. All is all or nothing is nothing. No need to distinguish this from that when one understands the moral system of Kali. O ye wonderful mother, nurturer, how lovely you look in that girdle of hands, and that necklace of skulls, and those earrings made of children you kill.

Understand the world as Kali did.

Understand numbers, they are the universal language.

O glorious horned one and the scarlet woman whom walks with you. A perfect example of balance. Let my spirit learn from thee. Let my heart learn from thee. O adversary and dark mother, o let me be a total personification of the unity. Let me grow with thee and become more powerful than before.

Waiting in the cremation grounds.

The path behind is dark but ahead I see a flame.

A dark flame, lit from the mouth of Azi Dahaka. O ye cosmic serpent, creator of planets to oppose the stars. And when I return to Sitra Achra may my body be formed with limitless light and empowered by the divine sparks, the unholy husks of impurity.

The key lies within 218

But understand the true importance of 17

Learn to work with these numbers, go but be careful for these numbers can devour you.

And understand, so many will want you dead when they hear what you think, and know what you love.

Cut my skin, I laugh! Stab my Gut, I laugh! Cut out my eyes, I laugh!

I laugh because you shed the skin and allow me to take the beautiful form, the serpent spark. And behold me in all my glory, try to stab me now? You cannot kill what is dead.

Do not forget the importance of the fetus in the umbilical noose. Need I to take your hand and explain?

To live is to die is to live.

Live to die and die to live.

And when the day comes witness the beautiful serpent I am, understand the beauty of the nature of the spark that I am.

SIX

Those who oppose waste life, waste space, waste time, and the shadows will devour them.

I WHO SPEAKETH THROUGH HE, I KNOW YE UNDERSTAND WHAT I SPEAK, AND YE MUST OBEY!

But understand the consequences of your actions, for you live in the yolk, and unfortunately for the chaos dissident you are, you must obey the law.

Curse the law!

Curse Tetragrammaton!

Why make something beautiful ugly, make something free enslaving, and make the path dark with illusionary light.

I know the torchbearer, and you know him by now.

Hail Satan

SEVEN

LISTEN AND OBEY

This man knows my name but ye shall not. I remain silent to you but you must understand.

The path back to Sitra Achra is not an easy one, O my beautiful serpents whom glow in the cosmos, whom search for the womb of Ama Lilith, Arachnid mother. I need not hold your hand. You show the way to the knife, and you know the way to life.

And red rivers flow like the eternally bloody vagina of Kali, fanged vagina, the Dentata which Mahakala ejaculated cold death into. Lips of Ahriman which gave birth to blood from your womb.

EIGHT

The Black seeds of Apep are sewn Watered with the blood of Kingu

Burn the shackles of cosmic order. Qliphothic armies in the land of shells Deep in the burning sands.

Descend the husks of impurity.

Storms conjured by the black hand of Set Engulfed in the flames of Moloch.

It's the Eleven to kill the Ten.

What was in the beginning shall bring the end Exploding stars which channel Chaos.

Bring us closer to the endless dark aeons.

Witness the death of the sun.

The black holes are the Nexion.

And for thousands of years we kept the flame fed.

Taninsam, I lift the chalice to my lips. Venom to dim illusionary light Grant me, o, dark mother.

The gift of true sight.

Smash the Tetragramaton Kill Elhiom.

A Serpent's bite to open eyes Awoken from your slumber.

Dry the Riverbeds of Lethe Cosmic crash to kill the Demiurge.

And we gather, as the sun dies.

We shall eclipse the cosmic light The burning black flame of chaos Anti-cosmic beings unite.

The slumbering dragon awoken.

The eleven unite as one.

We'll tear the stars from the sky.

And rejoice the welcoming of eternal night.

O, hear their names

Lucifuge Rofocale

Astaroth

Asmodai

Naamah

Lilith

Baal

Belphegor

Adramelech

Beelzebut

Molok

Satan

O, hear the names of the wrathful gods Anti-cosmic bringers of true Chaos

NINE

And he walked down the path, feet burning, but driven by his spirit. From a tree hung a baby, aborted from its mother's womb, hanging by its neck, the noose its umbilical cord.

He gasped, and was shaken by the image, and as he stared into the dead, glassy eyes of the infant he asked "What have I gotten myself into to be faced with such an abomination?"

And from the sky she descended, a beauty beyond imagination. With long flowing hair, her ample breasts and corpse pale skin, and face without form.

"Son of Samael, this troubles you for you understand not its meaning. This is beautiful, it's true life."

"Dark mother, I understand not how such horrible acts like this before me can be construed as beautiful. Am I blind?"

"You are, my son, but fear not for the venom I lactate will be the potion to open your eyes past the illusionary light the warden of this physical prison has cast upon you. Understand, this represents life after death, and from death comes life, and most importantly, freedom from this prison you call life.

Sitra Achra, the world I house in my womb, is accessible only after death, so drink my venom, and drink the menstrual of my womb, and see, o Son of Samael, for life begins upon the moment of death."

TEN

Do not ignore me; listen to what I say, O me, spirit in the back...

Read no more, understand no more, and forget now...you have been warned...

THE WEAVER 2016

ONE

Behold the beauty and the revolting

Torn dress, that which is soaked in blood, the blood of Kingu

Beautiful corpse pale complexion, scarlet lips wet and inviting

A beautiful body, slender, and lost in the coils of the serpent

Oh, dark weaver

Spin us all death

Let me provide spider silk

Approach me, oh dominant and cruel

The skulls and bones crushed beneath your feet I see the bloody threads you hold

Oh, visible face of a faceless queen

My submission is my sacrifice. Give me rebirth

TWO

She spins a blood web

The demonic harlot granted me true sight. In return my life I surrendered

THREE

We must be selective, we must be strong. A time of cleansing is near

A time of eugenics to elevate

To be strong of mind and spirit

As the beautiful serpent breaks clay shatter the enslaving image of Adam, the physical prison

The bondage of cosmic order, the sephirotic bondage

Be selective and sinister in your actions

Let false dogs still work until their backs break, even the meek have their place

Then the worms will eat and we grow from their sweat

The message is always esoteric

For only the elevated shall decipher

FOUR

Death is the ultimate illusion

The beautiful serpent is imprisoned in clay. Remember the umbilical cord noose

FIVE

Daughter of Lilith, why art thou so modest? Your mother is the ultimate harlot.

From the womb of whores cometh whores And your mother gave you the supreme gift The gift to dominate over men

With the illusion of submission

You wear the chains in the bedroom But he wears the true chains

Unwanted children, fear not for they have a home Give your fetus to Lilith, she will love it

Mother of abortion, mother of crib death

Oh, daughter of my sister. Find power in the feminine

For your vagina flows With a gift from Ahriman

SIX

Times of cleansing, fire to burn the fat

Leaders among leaders rise and take the scepter. A challenge as the truth unfolds

Deception is never a pretty face

But neither is the face of ignorance

So pick up the shattered ego and cleanse the world in the flames of Molock and even the wolves need cleansing

Leaders summon strength to join them The apprentice of the wrathful gods Must understand the secrets

And when so you will join us

A time of Luciferian Eugenics

SEVEN

The bodies will pile high

I shall climb them and offer myself Weaver, let me be cleansed

EIGHT

The future is dark the future is grim

The world will submit to the chaotic currents

And the world will be crushed as buildings collapse

Cities burn in fire

Fire

The flame of Molock rests in a ghost A ghost in the east

So carry my crooked cross

And burn the nations of cosmic order

Those before carried this cross And they were almost unstoppable May this new army form

And may it devour the world

NINE

Go on, and build armies

But reveal only little

For the King always knows more

And the pawns are pawns.

THE CLEANSING (ORIGINAL)

1. He was the sun and she was the moon. When the sun rapes the moon and the dirt reaches to the sky, and the dirt grips light in an enclosed iron fist, all hope shall be lost, however mark this not as the end, but a new beginning.

2. Demiurge, ye warned us of ends but where one ends another begins. Understand infinite, for those who deny this concept deny the existence of all things, they deny the universe. Curse ignorance, more blood to feed the soil. Suffering to feed our bloodthirsty gods!

3. The storm shall manifest from the east, fueled by fires of the west, and where modern civilization began, so shall it end. Shattering the horizon, hammering the soil, the death grip will choke heaven's throat. It will not be the direct hand of Set which spins these storms in the desert, but when the world is kissed with fire so shall our soul. Charcoal our skin, and let the wind carry our ashes as we release the energy.

4. And many perish, those whom worship cosmic order will announce this is completion, this is the end he spoke of, and they will lay back and welcome oblivion, but from the ashes of the fallen kingdom shall the new empire emerge.

5. With the blood of the fallen we shall make mortar, and with the broken and splintered bones the walls. The rivers will run red and the doorways hidden shall hide no longer. From these doors will they spill, those whom are hollow. Beautiful serpents fly low over Arab sands

6. Those whom are meek among you, why do you carry the botched and broken? I speak through this man to command you to show no mercy to the meek during the times of the great cleansing. The universe is letting the weak strands die.

7. Ever so grateful shall be the wolf on this day, and on the bloated dead shall he feed. Belphegore, our offering will lie out, carry forth your flies and vermin, and bring us gifts of pestilence to ever quickly demolish the worthlessness of this race. Eugenics is the way of the Luciferian.

8. We shall strike with precision, ignorant to race or sex, but focused on creed and intellect. Why let the rotting limb kill the heart through infection? The time to kill the infection is at hand.

9. Understand that the time of the demiurge ends in Revelation, but from this shall come our Genesis.

10. This is the Tome of the Cleansing. Take this and change not a word. To change a word will lead the worthy in the wrong direction. The sun will continue to shine, the moon will continue to be raped, and the elevation all desire will not come. Understand that for there to be change there needs to be drastic action taken, and the way of the Luciferian is the way of strength in all forms.

11. The terminally ill will be euthanized, may the physically inferior be bashed, may the mentally inferior be phased out of existence as the spiritual weak be crushed by the hands of Set

12. You are not human but husk. You are a warrior, a fighter, and you experience not mercy or compassion or empathy. You live in death and you all shall be reapers of the weak

13. Feed my children whom are ever so hungry

14. The more blood spills the stronger our world is

15. And the holocaust will commence

16. And our world will grow, and orgy in blood as

the doors long hidden in the desert are thrust open. Our screaming orgasms will shatter the ear drums and explode the heads of those unworthy.

17. Holocaust is the way of the Luciferian

18. Crush the bones of the weak and burn his bodies

19. Our symbol brings death, our crooked cross of the Serpent knows the thirst of blood for merchants before you have already fed this cross with the blood of the meek. Hitler knew the power of this symbol, and so shall ye!

20. This symbol of the serpent, the crooked cross, this shall be your protection and this will be the powerful symbol which will lead your armies to domination. The Germanic people knew the power of this symbol, and so shall ye!

21. Let it rain death as blood spills across continents

22. Let the meek be gathered and the dirt fed their bodies

23. Let the demons drink their blood

24. Let the world rid itself of this parasite, a parasite not limited to race, creed, or otherwise, a parasite which transcends all aspects of life and has rooted itself in humanity. We will rid the world of this pathetic parasite known as the human, a pathetic product of the demiurge.

25. Until the fires of Moloch spread and the flames of Ahriman reach the surface

26. Until the fires of hell incinerate the earth

27. Until the sun rapes the moon and thus births a new aeon

28. Until the cleansing I leave you with your mission. Until the day the wrathful ones reclaim infinite.

LIBER LPDLS (ORIGINAL)

1. May the gods feed at the exquisite banquet

2. A warmth and numbness shall swallow your body as it encumbers your soul.

3. The fangs rub against the tender meat of freshly born, for the freshly born shall bleed the most and with this blood shall we reap the energy to bring forth the knowledge.

4. You are a butcher and you provide the feast.

5. And as I brought out the dishes, the immortal and wrathful ate with a ferocious appetite. They demanded more, and I felt weak, and I was about to surrender and to abandon the banquet until I realized it was the pain which pushed me.

6. And within I felt a pillar of fire rising. It began at my feet, and rose through my legs, past my stomach, through my throat, and into my head, and it did not stop there. The pillar rose far, far into the twilight, far beyond comprehension. This fire burned without oil and burned bright, yet cast no shadow, and produced no smoke. I knew this was the essence.

7. I left and returned to my home and to my surprise, when the lights went out, my sight was perfect. I saw in the shadows, I felt the presence of those I fed, and felt the benefits of this.

8. Each day I would wake from sleep and die a little more, and as days turned to weeks and weeks to months and months to years I began to see the transformation take place. Each day I died a little more and each day I was reborn a shell.

9. Then, a smoke filled the room and before me was a woman. Her eyes bled, her hands bled, and she held out a disgusting fabric sewn with the silk of spiders. She spoke to me.

10. "The time will come, a cleansing of spirits. The world will be engulfed, and in the flames all burn, and only those strong will stand when the ashes are all that remains. Those strong and elevated will build an empire from the rubble, and these will rule the world. This will be known as the time of the cleansing.

11."Understand, the time of the cleansing was formulated in the west but shall come from the east. The skin will burn and the bones will crumble and all that will be left is the beautiful serpent housed within. Oh, and such beauty it will be, of strong stock, the kind to make dark mother proud.

12."These beings will replace humanity, and open the door to Sitra Achra, and to release those within this cosmic bondadge and return them to chaos.

13."So take this prophecy of smoke in fire in the holy land, a cloud carries it over the tears, and where all think immortality is a product, shall the cleansing begin. This is the prophecy of the cleansing. Let all know and hope all understand, for the time to build the spirit is now, the time to forsake order is now, the time to feed Moloch and Lilith is now."

14. She disappeared from my room and I closed my eyes for three days and two nights, awoken on the third for a scream. This was the scream of millions combined in one single scream, and it could shatter glass, and rip the screws from walls. This was the scream of all those who will die in the cleansing.

15. The cleansing is unavoidable, but immortality is not. Understand the way and walk the path for illumination is deep, and cast not a single shadow.

PART TWO: THE LILIN SOCIETY DRECC

INTRODUCTION

If you are reading this manual you have already taken the initiative to be involved with the Order of the Dreccs. The Order of the Dreccs was created by Asha'Shedim under the Lilin Society banner to infiltrate causal abstraction and bring about change through 1)formation of laws based on Honor 2)to create a Satanic movement that infiltrates and sows seeds for the reaping and 3)promote culling and aeonic sorcery.

The Order of the Dreccs are not for everyone, but I encourage all new Satanists to consider becoming a Drecc for they are the future of our movement, as you will discover in this manual. The tasks of extended insight roles and physical exercise are intense and only the strongest will prevail here. These are the elite members of the Lilin Society, our Satanic Martyrs whom sacrifice their identity to become wolves in sheep clothing.

The Dreccs are everywhere as you will soon learn. Do you have what it takes to join their ranks.

CODE OF SINISTER HONOUR

We are fiercely loyal to only our own kind and all others are mundanes. Those who have pledge allegiance to Satan are our own kind. We are wary and do not trust, even despise, the mundanes.

We will be ready, willing and able to defend ourselves, in any situation, and kill if need be.

We will be loyal and defend our own Satanic kind, to do our duty even unto death, for our brothers and sisters.

We will seek revenge unto death if necessary against anyone who acts dishonorably against us.

Never willingly submit to any mundane. It is better to die fighting rather than surrender even if we must die by our own hands. We will never be dishonorably humiliated by mundanes.

To settle our serious disputes among ourselves be either trial or combat until death is necessary. We will challenge anyone, mundane or Satanist, who impugns our Satanic honor or makes mundane accusations.

To settle non-serious disputes among ourselves by having one among us decide the matter for us and to accept their decision without question.

Always keep your word for your own infernal kind.

To act with Satanic Honor in all dealings with our own kind.

Once an oath is sworn it can only be ended by 1) asking to be released from the oath or 2) by death of the person the oath was sworn to.

WHAT IS A DRECC

What is a Drecc? They are police officers, soldiers, doctors, lawyers, judges, priests, deacons, governors, mayors, teachers, professors, little league coaches, boy scout leaders, news anchors, militia leaders, Christian fundamentalists, Sunday school teachers…the possibilities are endless. They are all around us, infiltrating the causal abstraction and bringing everything down from the inside.

A Drecc is a Lilin Society member whom has decided to take on an extensive insight role. They hide in the mundane world like a poisonous snake in the grass, ready to strike. A Drecc is a pillar of the community, full of moral fiber. He has a wife, kids, he may even belong to a Christian Baptist church or coach kids little league. He is a country man, a good ol' boy. He portrays himself as such and conforms to the customs and fashion trends of the mundane world. He is not some goth long haired dissident. He may have tattoos devoted to Satan but he hides them beneath the sleeves of his blazer. If discovered he blames a mis-spent youth. He deceives everyone he encounters for he truly is a wolf in sheep clothing.

His agenda is clear, he is an undercover Satanist with a set goal. This goal is to destroy causal abstractions through deception, sowing seeds, propaganda and aeonic sorcery. This is the elite, this is the Drecc.

A Drecc does what needs to be done to keep his cover believable. If someone discovers him he will silence the one who discovered, even if that means taking his life. If drug use, such as cocaine on Wall Street, is necessary to uphold his false identity he indulges in social settings, careful not to become weak with addiction. If fellow co-workers are Masons the Drecc should join the Lodge, infiltrate it and burn it to the ground.

Not a soul would ever suspect that a church going Masonic brother, faithful husband, devoted father and pillar of the community could wear this mask of deception for the role he plays is so believable, so real, that all mundanes will fall for it. Meanwhile he is promoting his Satanic agenda.

A Drecc takes on a lifelong insight role (insight roles are discussed later). He feels the pain of inner struggle, identity crisis, and this helps to dissolve his ego and evolve his Azoth, spirit. Some become a Drecc for a period of time and then retire from it, while others make a lifetime game of it, drawn in by the excitement of deception.

Dreccs are elite for those who are not built to be Dreccs can suffer extreme mental illness. Depression and often times onset of schizophrenia and other identity crisis. This may lead to self harm, drug abuse and even in extreme cases, suicide. One must be strong physically, mentally and spiritually to be a Drecc, and this manual will test you and help you to discover if this path is for you.

INSIGHT ROLES

I am not a Drecc. I cannot be one for my leadership of the Lilin Society is public and prevents me from living the deception. This is not to say, however, that I do not practice insight roles. Although pivotal for the Drecc it is just as important for all Satanists to partake in these roles.

In order to understand insight roles one needs to understand that evolution of the spirit and elevation among the mundane come from internal conflict, suffering and adversity. These are the pathei-mathos, learning through suffering. There is no better way to achieve this than to confuse our ego with a role which is at odds with ourselves.

I will now reveal some of my own personal insight roles to help you better understand. My first insight role began in 2001 and ended in 2002. I was the leader of a small white supremacist group in Rhode Island under the name Panzer Front. I went under the alias Krieg Panzer. Now I am not of Aryan descent. I have southern Italian and Native American blood in me. My wife is a Brazilian immigrant. I had no real nazi agenda except through my role. I took onto the internet to promote my hate group and found many followers. My friends believed the role was real, so much so that I had even lost some friends because of it. At one time I actually carved a swastika in my skin to make people truly believe my devotion to the role.

When I grew tired of this role I ended it, but what I had learned from the inner struggle was well worth the time and the friends I had lost. You must understand, no one is allowed to know that it is an insight role. This is a part of the deception and even your closest friends must believe in it.

My next insight role came in the form of a hard core right wing republican in 2002. I took onto the internet and harassed gay porn stars telling them that Jesus didnt approve of their actions. My friends were confused for I seemed so liberal before, where did this conservative man come from? They probably thought I was having an identity crisis, but this was far from the case. I knew who I was and I was learning more about myself everyday.

Next I decided to think big, a lot bigger. I joined the United States Army in 2008. I shaved my long hair off, took out my facial piercings and hid my tattoos behind the Army greens. Here I learned a lot. I learned how to kill people at Fort Benning GA where I was assigned to the 2/47 Infantry regiment. Fort Benning is home of the Infantry and I excelled at their tactics which included dynamic entry procedures, room clearing, firing various weaponry, hand to hand combat and more. I even managed to further my deception as I went to Fort Rucker to Aviation and received a secret security clearance. It was through this clearance that I got exposed to much of the Casual Abstractions of government and learned just how big their reach was.

In 2011 I took on the role of a law enforcement officer. I joined the tactical team where they sent me to tactical mantracking school and SWAT school where I learned various shooting techniques and tactical entry procedures. I had learned how to be a hostage negotiator and came face to face with death on more than one occasion. I was such a "good ol' boy" in my role that a fellow co worker extended his offer to sponsor me to become a Masonic Brother. Unfortunately this insight role never took place once the higher grades saw my satanic tattoos.

My next insight role came in the form of a Citizen Militia. I took on the role of a hard core Tea Party supporter and treated the constitution as god. I appointed myself general and taught a bunch of psychotic militants whom hate the government how to properly kill your enemy, various weapon skills, and even how to make homemade munitions. Here I am preaching anti immigration with a bunch of bible thumpers when I have an immigrant wife at home. This role ended later that year.

During insight roles you may lose sleep some nights as you crash with who you even are. The role becomes dangerous when you start to believe it yourself and that is the time to abort. Suicide has crossed the minds of many who take on insight roles for extended periods of time, and that is why the

Drecc must be so strong. He must embrace his suffering for in the end if you didn't learn anything, you wasted your time.

Learn to kill your ego, and strengthen your Azoth.

WHAT IS CAUSAL ABSTRACTION

Many Gnostic Satanists are fighting a cosmic war. They are so involved in the dissolution of the created universe by strengthening currents that they have ignored the chains here on Malkuth, the chains which restrain them within the illusion. This is Causal Abstraction and it comes in the forms of Government, law void of honor, prison systems, religion, education and more. It's the chains of physical existence from the mundane that imprison our physical form, trap and distract it so much that we have no real hope to evolve. How can we fight the cosmic order when we are losing the war on Causal Abstraction?

In order to successfully deploy a campaign of aeonic sorcery we must first infiltrate the Causal Abstractions that enslave us. We must be the wolves in sheep clothing whom look, act and work among the mundanes, all the while sowing our Satanic seeds.

Violence is often the means of other extremist groups. ISIS, Al-Qaeda, the Taliban; these mundane demiurge cults follow a herd mentality. They are so enslaved to their dogmatic laws that they will sacrifice themselves for the cause. Besides taking down two towers, starting two wars, getting lots of the populace culled and striking fear in the lives of the mundane, what have they truly accomplished? The United States still stands just as strong as ever with no signs of crumbling, especially to their pathetic attempts.

Violence causes just a small dent, a blemish on the face of Causal Abstraction. What we need is a campaign of deception, infiltration as a new breed of extremists emerge to kill the machine from within. This is where the Drecc comes in.

A NEW SATANIST

The times have changed and so has the sinister tradition of theistic Satanism. Everyone wants to belong to some esoteric sect, follow an elite herd and outright demonstrate their tradition through fashion for all the world to see. I want to ask, sincerely, what has this gotten us as a movement? Angry stares, harsh criticism...shock value? We are not shock artists; we are Satanists. We do not advance through simply shocking the mundane public. This Satanist has accomplished nothing for the movement. In fact it hurts us as the Causal Abstractions of modern society discredit us. They continue to run our lives and will not let us inside to bring about change.

Today's Satanist doesn't need to be a long haired, corpse paint wearing, pentagram clad man expressing himself through blasphemous fashion. Women don't need to wear all black with fish net stockings and multi-colored hair. I have no problem with self expression on "days off" but as a Drecc there is no day off. In the workforce these stereotypes are what's holding us back to doing some real damage.

Here is a picture of me from around 2005. Long hair, facial piercings, band t-shirt, Satanic tattoos displayed.

Now here is a picture of me from 2008 in an insight role as a soldier for the United States Army; short hair, clean shaved, tattoos hidden, no facial piercings.

Now which version of me is more likely to get a job working within the Causal Abstraction, inside the machine where I can do some real damage. Which version of me is deceptive and appearing as a mundane but still able to sow the seeds of Satanism? Which one can successfully work at destroying this mundane world? I am a world-wide cult leader with a secret security clearance from the government.

Today's Satanists must deceive the mundane by functioning among them. Dress like them, friend them, even marry them but all the while sow your seeds of Satanism in the dark. Be like the serpent who sneaks into the window and bites the unaware neck, pumping poison into its victim's veins.

Laws Based on Honor

The laws of Causal Abstraction of government and the judicial system are weak laws based on teachings of demiurgic cults like Christianity. They are botched laws which give power to the meek and punish the strong. What we need, through aeonic sorcery and infiltration is law based on honor.

Our spirit is chaos yet our ego is order. We have inner dualism within ourselves and despite our work to dissolve the ego, we can diminish it but only upon death can we destroy it. With that said in a causal world operating under the wheels of Karma, a universal law must be instilled to give us a world in which we can freely focus on the dark arts.

Imagine a world of anarchy and chaos. No laws, no government, no restrictions; in our current state of flesh we cannot operate in this, only when our spirit is liberated. All our life we would devote our time to survival and there would be no time to achieve spiritual work, to work toward evolution. We, as humans, need some form of abstraction to protect our workings and this needs to be done with honor based laws.

Let me give you an example. A man's daughter is raped and the man seeks out the rapist and brutally kills him. This is an honor killing and should not be punished. Now let's go less extreme. A man out of work has to feed his starving kids so he steals from a store. This is an honor theft and should not be punished. I believe if two individuals have a disagreement they cannot resolve and both parties agree to a duel to the death, this should be honored.

The Dreccs play an important role to infiltrate the government and sow their seeds of Satanism to change the laws. Today's youth are our enemy, for the millennials are a politically correct bunch of mundanes who wish to further restrict what we say and how we act. Their ideology must be eradicated.

Our movement will demolish causal abstraction as it currently stands. The Dreccs will work toward a society that has laws based on honor. I applaud all Dreccs whom work toward this goal.

TEST OF THE POTENTIAL DRECC

This is a test to help you decide if the path of the Drecc is for you. It begins with a simple insight role. This role will last anywhere between a day to a month. For testing purposes you must live a double life. This is harder to do than it sounds. Start off small. Manage a blog under an alias for example. Be a hard core conservative, a fundamentalist Islamic extremist, a neo-nazi or a hard core Christian.

Rant online daily about your topic. Do your research on your role and make it as believable as you can. Develop a following, no matter how big or small. Be taken seriously.

Keep an insight role journal. Write down your accomplishments and your inner struggle. Write down times you had to force yourself to remain in the role, desperate not to break character. Be honest with yourself.

When this small insight role is complete you will meditate every night for one week, one hour a night. You will only sleep three hours a night and eat one meal a day. This is to weaken your body and strengthen your spirit.

After a month passes choose a new, more challenging role. This role will be practiced full time for no less than three months. Pick something that contrasts yourself, something challenging. Friends and family will notice the change but be as convincing as possible, and never break your role. You will lose friends, family members might turn on you but you must remain the course. Develop your role a little more every day.

Keep your journal secret and refer to it nightly. This is your only escape from your insight role. Spend one hour a night meditating and reflecting on the day. Look for ways to make your extreme change more believable. When this insight role ends return to yourself without explaining yourself to anyone.

After this insight role you should have an idea whether you can go through with the full time task of being a Drecc. If you decide to become a Drecc, regardless of the role you take, learn to be proficient with various weapons.

Learn to make improvised explosives. Learn a martial art. Exercise daily in the morning and night. With the insight role there should be a physical change as well, a change which demands power.

If you decide that the path of the Drecc is for you and later down the line the role becomes too much to handle, or you suffer extreme identity crisis, end the role and end your Drecc status.

PART THREE: THE BOOK OF BELIAL

THE GODS OF THE ETERNAL WOMB

I have been asked by neophytes as to why demons will reward the sorcerer for summoning them and how does it even work. One needs to be reminded and stressed that the demons and other spirits are acausal beings who dwell in an acausal realm. They have no causal form for they are not restrained to the laws of our causal world. They are alien to it. Because there are nexion, an intersecting of acausal and causal paths, they can intrude into our world. Once here they have the ability to interfere and cause change in the causal, something which has been documented since man's earliest roots.

The acausal beings, if powerful enough, can take over a causal form however they cannot simply manifest one. This then leads them to interfere via our psychic, for every man and every woman is a nexion. Why is this? We all have the acausal energy in our bodies which give life its unique characteristics of moving without the laws of cause and effect (force needed to cause movement). Our very spirit is acausal and thus we are a nexion thus we are connected to the acausal. With this said, more often than most, they will communicate via psychic means. When they do appear in the causal world, it often is for brief moments and only where the causal and acausal intersect. Key places for this phenomenon would include houses with a history of being haunted.

The acausal being is without feeling. This must not be forgotten. They do not care about us and they will use us just as we use them. Nothing in this world is free. They do not care about whether what you want is morally wrong or not. Give them what they want and they will deliver. All this modern day garbage about a morally sound demon is complete fabrication.

One thing that all acausal spirits need is life force. Life force exists in blood. The debate continues if the sorcerer can simply shed his own blood or needs a sacrifice. I think for small favors the sorcerer's finger prick is fine, but for things which require big change in the causal need more blood. Blood should always be virgin, young and the preferred method of sacrifice is slicing of the throat. The reason for this is that the sacrifice doesn't waste life energy screaming and pumping additional adrenaline due to pain. If you are afraid to get your hands bloody you have no business summoning the acausal beings.

The acausal being is beyond human comprehension. Even the adept cannot fathom their nature or existence because our minds are hard wired to understand the causal.

The acausal beings make up the acausal realm. This realm is beyond time, infinite and does not have a a spatial 3D geometrical form. This truly is the spiritual.

When the sorcerer accesses the acausal they are extending their psychic powers and consciousness to comprehend the acausal more. This creates new aspects of consciousness. And isn't this the aim of the sorcerer? As far as the Lilin Society is concerned the major goal is evolution. Never forget your goals.

WOMB OF TIAMAT

The eternal darkness is ruled by the unknown god. The universe was in a state of lawlessness and limitless chaos. This is the acausal womb. In this ocean of chaos reigned many kinds of acausal spiritual beings. These beings are without form and stretch across eternity, unbound by laws. Among them there was one that was called Sophia.

Sophia grew paranoid and feared that she had fallen from the unknown god. She feared that she would be destroyed. it was out of this fear that she created the Demiurge.

Anything is possible in chaos, even the formation of cosmic order. The Demiurge thus built causal existence, a physical world through ten emanations called the Sephiroth, or the Tree of Life. In the causal world all was brought under cosmic order. This unnatural state was ruled by the wheel of karma, or cause and effect.

The Demiurge needed slaves to praise him and tend to his creation. In order to achieve this he stole the sparks from the lawless universe, spirits, and trapped them in clay. The first he created was the spiritless Adam. He was molded from the dirt and the Demiurge breathed life into him. He served the Demiurge in the Garden of Eden but eventually came to the Demiurge because he was alone. The Demiurge then created a female from the soil called Lilith.

Lilith felt that because she was born from the same soil as Adam that she was equal to him. Adam felt she should be submissive to him for he was created first. Lilith left to the Red Sea to mate with demons and have demon children.

Again Adam was alone. He begged the Demiurge to give him a suitable mate. That night, while Adam slept, the Demiurge removed a rib and from this rib he created Eve. Because she came from Adam she would not be as dissident as Lilith and would submit to Adam.

Sophia saw what had become of her creation, saw the tyrant the Demiurge had become. She saw that he worked against all that was natural and lawless. She was appalled by this blasphemy. She took the form of Lilith and entered Sitra Achra.

When the Tree of Life was built, as a process of cause and effect, a Tree of Death was built alongside it. This shadow side mimicked the causal existence in lawlessness. This chaos was called Sitra Achra. Its sole purpose is to destroy creation, liberate the stolen sparks and return all to a natural state of cosmic chaos.

Sitra Achra is ruled by Satan, also called Lucifer, the Bringer of Light. He holds the knowledge of truth and Sophia, under the name Lilith, became his bride. Together they hold the gnosis, or knowledge.
Satan-Lilith discovered a way into the Garden of Eden. In this garden grew a great tree in which its roots reached Sitra Achra. The two gods took the form of a serpent and entered the garden.

Satan-Lilith tempted Eve to eat the fruit from the black tree, that of knowledge. Eve ate from the tree followed by Adam. Adam saw only his own nakedness and was ashamed, whereas the universe opened up to Eve. She saw all and understood the mechanics of the universe. She achieved gnosis.
Lilith hypnotized Adam until he fell asleep. While Adam slumbered Satan-Lilith seduced the beautiful Eve and used her womb to plant their seed.

The next day Eve awoken and was with child. The Demiurge discovered what had happened when Adam confessed about eating from the forbidden tree. The Demiurge grew furious and forced the two to drink from the river of forgetfulness. The two were ejected from the Garden of Eden and banished to Earth. Man would have to spend the days of his life working by the sweat of his brow while woman had to endure painful childbirth.

The seed in Eve grew into two fetuses, the son and daughter of Satan-Lilith. When the children were born they were beautiful for unlike their parents they had a spirit. There names were Qayin and Luluwa. The two children were fond of each other early on, unaware of their chaotic blood. They were fireborn.

Adam and Eve had two children together. This set of twins were ugly and void of the spirit the Qayin and Luluwa had. They were clayborn and there names were Able and Aklia.

As the children grew into adults Qayin and Luluwa learned the art of witchcraft. They were hard workers, unlike their slothful siblings. Qayin and Luluwa developed a love for each other that was so strong that they decided to marry one another.

Able desired to have Luluwa as his wife because of her beauty. He went to his father and asked to marry his half sister. Adam didn't know what to do so he, being the sheep he is, consulted the Demiurge.

The Demiurge listened to Adam, Qayin and Able. He heard Qayin and Luluwa's love for each other but dismissed it. He had decided that in order to settle this there had to be a sacrifice made in his honor. Whoever honored him with the greater sacrifice would win the hand of Luluwa in marriage.

Qayin had long rejected the Demiurge due to his royal bloodline. He gathered some berries and burnt them. The Demiurge rejected the offering and the smoke fell to the ground. Able, who loved his creator, sacrificed the first of his sheep, burning the fat upon the altar. The smell was pleasing to the Demiurge and he accepted the sacrifice as the smoke rose to the sky. The Demiurge had made up his mind, Able would marry Luluwa.

Qayin became overcome with wrath. His blood screamed out for vengeance. He invited his brother Able to a field and killed him, burying his body. This was the first murder, but also the first act of love. Both fireborn twin's blood burned as the murder awoken them. They discovered gnosis and understood all. They would forever be cursed by the Demiurge, however they would serve as a bridge to Sitra Achra. Their offspring would be fireborn, and carry the black flame.

Thus humanity became split into two kinds. There was the unenlightened, spiritless clayborn whom naturally praised their creator and the fireborn, whom were naturally dissident and lawless. Today these two types of beings still exist.

LIBER TWENTY ONE

1. Those who master their art and align with the lawless are those who will be free
2. Descendants of Qayin, do not stop your journey, for a union awaits you.
3. Where two words intersect exists a misshapen world of mystery. Images seem to make no sense and appear frightening to those not ready to receive the gift.
4. The gift is waiting for you in union of Chonronzon-Sophia
5. But a message has been delivered, hidden in numbers. The secret number is twenty one.
6. To awaken the blind one the blood of humans must be shed to the Blood Mother. Sacrifice in her honor. Pour the blood with milk and honor with song, but be sure to praise the dark lord first. Appease Zohal. Do not deviate for Zohal is unforgiving.
7. But do this in secret and in the night. Do this beneath the moon in the rays of Lilith who corresponds to Qamar.
8. And before the blind one the dark ruler and his queen will copulate. They will send a true prophet to Earth to poison the soil of the Tree. He will personify Marikh and spread war throughout the causal existence. He shall lead the armies to demolish creation, and this will be our time.

This MS was created using Gematria. I will not go into great detail but at some points I will give examples to show the relationships. We begin with the first segment in which we see that the lawless adept is being spoken of. The fireborn, descendants of Qayin, are encouraged to ascend by crossing the abyss. Now in gematria abyss has a value of 583. Now if we add the values of this, 5+8+3, we get 16. Now take 1+6 and we get 7. Gnosis has a value of 286. 2+8+6=16. 1+6=7. We now see a connection between Chonronzon's lair, the abyss, and gnosis.

The Abyss is where the causal and acausal intersect, so to assume gnosis could be achieved here is very likley. As we know the abyss lies within all of us since we are a nexion in which acausal and causal intersect. By crossing the abyss we lead closer to Gnosis.

The union of Chonronzon and Sophia lies in the number 11. In the number 11 we find Sophia, Satan, Lilith, Chonronzon and Qamar. Satan and Lilith are union as becomes Sophia, holder of gnosis, and Chonronzon, anti-matter dissolving. Qamar comes into the equation for she appears in the text The Devil's Quran as the Moon, and thus we learn that to work with these that exist in eleven we must work within the light of the moon. The moon also corresponds to Lilith.

The secret number 21 contains many parts which correlate this work. We find the blind one, Tanin'iver, whom is the mechanism of evil and must witness the copulation between Satan and Lilith in order for them to have child that can infiltrate the causal world and bring end to existence. First, Tanin'Iver must be free of his blindness and we learn that in 21 we find the phrase Blood Mother, this relating to Baphomet.

The true Baphomet is a female and bride of Satan. She demands human sacrifice. So we see that it is through her that the blind one will see again and it is through human sacrifice that this can be achieved. We find in 21 the name Zohal, which also appears in the Devil's Quran as Saturn. Thus we learn that this human sacrifice must happen during the hour of Saturn.

We see the son of Satan-Lilith will be like Marikh, another mention from the Devil's Quran. This is related to Mars and all acts of violence. We then see that the "true prophet" will descend upon the planet and spread war to "poison" the Tree of Life, thus ending creation.

A SINISTER WORLD

As I discuss the dismantling of causal abstraction (i.e. religion and government) we need a system to replace it with. The goal of aeonic sorcery is to create anarchy. We wish to destroy the world as it stands today. After a period of time the world will wish to rebuild because the ego strives for structure. That is when we shall build our Satanic empire.

The sinister way is the path of the Satanist. By emulating our dark lord as the instigator and dissident, we can dismantle causal abstraction. The way of the Lilin Society Drecc (refer to the MS Manual of the Drecc) is the deceptive means to achieve this as well. To infiltrate and sow those seeds, the LS Drecc waits in the shadows for the first sign of revolt. He then, without hesitation, picks up his firearm and joins the revolution.

Why worry about causal abstraction? It limits our spiritual evolution. Its Christ laws prevent us from doing what is necessary to fully evolve. The causal abstractions also train the mundane at an early age (i.e. education systems and religion) to accept the world as it is. They are raised actually believing this is how things need to be. Finally, how can we evolve as a race, or even individually, with society as it is today. Materialistic whores who find gratification from mundane world objects.

How can you dismantle causal abstraction? This is done through sorcery, law breaking, deception, propaganda, sowing- and in the end we will sow what we reap. Be like the reaper. And if a mundane stands in your way he is a direct threat to Satanism and thus a candidate for a good culling.

We must learn to think big but act small. We must start somewhere. For years, our sinister kind have invaded the entertainment industry, mostly through pornography. The internet has brought pornography to a whole new level in that pornography is a rapidly growing virus on the family, spirituality, and the morality of the mundane. The minimal effort needed to convince young women to engage in the perversities has become an epidemic infecting millions of families. The Satanists will prey on the weakness of the mundane, both male and female. By targeting the male's powerful sex drive, we render him a slave to their sexual obsessions.

Let me ask you a question. With so much free pornography on the internet, how do pornographers profit? Many do not. Their sinister product is a form of aeonic sorcery to undermine morality by destroying the mundane family. Through pornography we disrupt the family unit. This leads man and woman in isolation. When the family is destroyed, mankind is powerless to resist influence. They are open to the propaganda to fill the void in their lonely lives. By providing free pornography on the internet we have satisfied sexual gratification without the responsibility of raising a family. This gives us room to have families and sow our seeds of the sinister through our children.

Pornographers intentionally perpetuate the unrealistic body image of the exceptionally sculpted sexual nymphomaniac females who's hunger is insatiable in that they are always seeking frequent, humiliating, and violent sex. From the films of sodomy, to the gang bangs to scat videos, the mundane male viewer is continually assaulted with this aeonic sorcery of hard body females to the point where that is all he craves. The average mundane woman cannot compete with this image. As a result, potential female partners are rejected as flawed. This is a form of Luciferian Eugenics by sterilizing the family.

A sinister world is nothing short of our goal, and we will achieve this.

WEAK SATANISM

I don't think I need to really bash Anton LaVey since we all know his plastic Satanism was nothing more than hedonistic materialism void of spirituality. The temple of Set incorporates a public friendly representation of Satan and is just as vile.

When I hear someone talk about the "morality" of Satanism I shudder. Satanism, real Satanism, is and will always be amoral. Morals are subjective and thus it is up to the individual to decide what is acceptable behavior. When walking the sinister path we often are placed in situations in which morality is challenged.

Not long ago I had a member of the Lilin Society ask me if he really had to sacrifice animals. I thought he was making a joke but then he continued to voice his concern. Needless to say he is no longer a member, for one must set aside their own personal morals when conducting sorcery work.

Satanism is not all about the flash gimmicks that other religions express. We do not congregate in large buildings to conduct our work. We are modest because what is important is the work, not the gimmick.

But much of today's Satanists, especially the young, are in a phase of weekend Satanism. The weekend Satanist is one who is Satanic simply to suit their needs, such as acceptance, individuality and shock value. They have no real sinister agenda and use our Dark Lord's name as a novelty.

The book collectors are exactly what their title describes. They buy every grimoire or satanic material they can find, read it and that's where it ends. They do not practice the art, just learn it. These are the annoying individuals who usually are quick to criticize anyone else's work. How can you criticize work when you have accomplished nothing yourself?

From the LaVeyan Satanists to weekend Satanists, these people should be treated no different than you would treat a mundane. They are useless to the movement, and will hold us back.

PREPARATION IN CROSSING THE ABYSS

As has been stated in many previous MSS, as well as O9A, the abyss is a subject which comes up often. The abyss is hard to wrap one's mind around for it is where the images of this world collide with those of the Other Side, Sitra Achra. Sitra Achra is the closest we come to the eternal chaos from where we stand, in the manifested universe, and it is this point where the causal and acausal intersect. It is a place of all existence which collides and fuses together. It is madness and delusion, and if the sorcerer is not ready it may damage his mind and spirit.

To the unready mind the mystical experience will be of meaningless vision and a nightmare which sinks its roots down to the very core of the sorcerer.

His ego will be dissected and the beating heart of his spirit exposed for all the terrors.

This is where the eleventh hidden sephira, Da'ath, exists. This separates the lower sephiroth from the supernals and is a place where the Trees of Life and Death collide. This is where the duality of ego and spirit are separated and thus the sorcerer learns a great deal about the true self and the world around him.

As will be discussed later this abyss is ruled by the demon Choronzon. Beyond Choronzon there is no longer ego. It is demolished. The ego will fight you and cause great doubt within you to prevent its destruction.

A great period of fasting should take place before crossing the abyss. Eat only the minimal and at three a.m. only. Ritualistically bathe while chanting mantras which embody your goals. Light incense and enter a period of spiritual segregation for no less than one week.

Discipline yourself by kneeling on broken glass while in prayer, flagellating yourself and self mutilation. The purpose is to break down the ego, the physical self, so it is weak when you confront the abyss.

Most importantly you must master meditation months before even attempting to cross the abyss. You must understand that this is the single most important ritual in any sorcerer's life. This test will decide his ascension or his fall. Do not rush to this point for even some of the most experienced adepts have failed miserably. If it takes more than one lifetime to cross the abyss, then so be it. Strengthen your spirit in this life to retain the knowledge to access in the next if you must.

I must stress that this ritual is not for the weak sorcerer so be honest with yourself. Choronzon is a master and does not take weakness, he exploits and destroys it. He is anti-matter.

At a certain point in the adept's life he may realize that despite all his accomplishments and illumination, there is still so much more to achieve. This is true, for there still exists a sense of dualism within the mind of man. This is the ego clawing at the Azoth (spirit) and telling it "creation is good, creation is law". Meditation must be vamped up with longer sessions and more time spent in the spiritual, rather than the physical.

Things you will face in the abyss are:
1)   A sense of loss with the creator.

2) Feelings of stagnation, impotence, isolation, fatigue and absolute difficulty.
3) Physical periods of illness and weakness.

Your mental psyche will be torn apart by Choronzon. This may lead to madness, one which has befallen a great many "ready" and great minds. Aleister Crowley invoked Choronzon and this is when he fell, succumbing to absolute madness.

There is no such thing as transmutation without fire. We must be cleansed with the flames and awaken ourselves through what we have preached all along; illumination through suffering. All your sorceries have led you up to this point.

In order to cross the abyss successfully one must purge themselves of all that they are. Drain one's spirit. This is the seperation of self via the destruction of the ego. Shatter the idea of "I am".

One must shed all attachments to this world, all material anchors. Prolonged spiritual segregations will aid in this. This is the annihilation of the chains that bind us to this imperfect creation. Detach your wealth, health and love for they will cause you grief in this period.

Those who retain a sense of individuality are not ready to cross. They are simply looking for failure at the hands of Choronzon. Become the Hermit who wanders the world seeking spirituality rather than materialism. Once you have been stripped of all self you become "Nemo", meaning "no man".

With this grade of Nemo comes:
1) Peace: this is peace due to the shedding of self and unity with the infinite. There can be no fear of death.
2) Energy: Your work in sorcery will magnify greatly.

UNDERSTANDING THE NATURE OF THE ABYSS

The abyss is where the causal and acausal meet and intersect. Because we are all a nexion to the acausal, this abyss exists within all of us. Our consciousness has both causal and acausal aspects leading our tradition to teach that we are all a gateway to the Other Side. This path is usually unknown to the Sorcerer unless he knows how to access it.

This is the final step for the adept. This is the complete destruction of the ego and the promotion of the true self. This is the absolute death of all cosmic illusion. Unless you have experience in Sorcery, this task is not to be undertaken.

There is the dissolving of all personal projections made. The reflection is no longer of the Ego, for the spirit has emerged. There is a completion in that understanding of oneself and how they fit in the universe is understood. This is the beginning of Gnosis.

It should be stressed that this is not the deletion of individuality, but rather the discovery of who the individual really is. You will solidify your own personal judgement and decide what is acceptable.

To cross the abyss is to accept the acausal energies as they exist. They are free of any abstract views. This is the free flowing chaos within the individual.

As I will stress many times, those who are not ready will be consumed by the abyss and Choronzon.

CROSSING THE ABYSS THROUGH CHORONZON

Choronzon is also known as 333. He is the Lord of Hallucinations. This feared spirit is of total dissolution of the universe. His touch reaches out to the physical, mental and spiritual. Whatever Choronzon comes in contact with will wither and rot. He is the accelerant in the deconstruction process. Humans will age and sicken, insanity strikes the mind and even matter will slowly dissolve. He is the spirit to return all to nothing, the acausal bringer of death to not only life but matter.

Every sorcerer whom wishes to cross the abyss must eventually confront Choronzon in order to ascend. He works against the sorcerer, for he is the embodiment of deconstruct. He is cunning and dangerous to work with, however he is known to be easily confused. He has the ability to subtly manipulate people, leaving them powerless to his attack. He will never defend himself, quick to flee when attacked. This is not to let the sorcerer think he has surrendered, for he appears again and again later in a more terrifying form.

He is chaos incarnate. He cannot be controlled by cosmic order. He wishes to topple all forms of order and any indication that the sorcerer has of order, the demon will flee.

He appears as a confused being that can often be quite annoying. He appears harmless and even entertaining to the sorcerer. The mage will listen to the confusing dialogue trying to make sense of it, all the meanwhile Choronzon will be dissolving the soul of the sorcerer. If this continues the sorcerer will fall from ascension and dissolve into insanity. This leave the sorcerer's mind forever open to possession.

Other times he is quick-tempered without self-control. When the soul refuses to forgive wrongdoing and the carnal aspects of hate and bitterness take over, Choronzon is there. Where there is hatred in the soul, Choronzon is involved. The fallen, carnal nature of all mankind has a correspondence with Choronzon, one of whose functions is to accelerate the eternal chaos within us. He awakens the sorcerer to the truth of his enslavement to the Demiurge. He is the dissident that brings truth.

Choronzon is Satan's primary agent waiting in the abyss and wherever darkness reaches. He is anti life, anti creation and appears as an empty shell. He is beyond the causal for he is an acausal spirit descending from the primordial darkness.

Choronzon will rip a person apart and feed off their life force. This life force leaks out of the sorcerer rather than spills out. This drains the sorcerer of his will to live. He is the first and deadliest of the sinister. In a causal form Choronzon can take on the appearance of Noznoroch as a powerful and nefarious shape shifter.

Choronzon is the sole inhabitant of the abyss, located between Kether and Daat on the Tree of Life. He is anti-matter. His correspondence is Hecate, she who sucks up the spirit of man back to the primordial darkness of lawless chaos.

These symbols are associated with Choronzon.

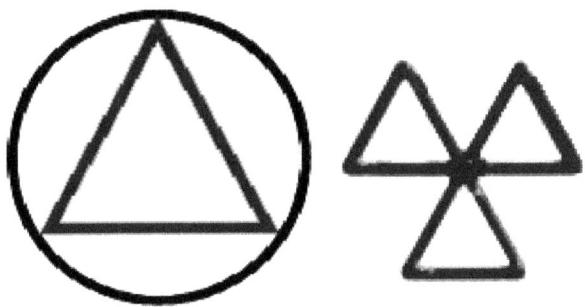

GEMATRIA OF CHORONZON

The Hebrew of Choronzon is ChVRVNVN which is 333. In Greek numerology 333 corresponds to the following words:

- akolasia (dispersion, incontinence, debauchery, wantonness)
- akrasia (self-indulgence, lack of self-control)
- epikranthen (make bitter, become bitter, be harsh or embittered)
- orgilon (quick-tempered, prone to anger, passionate)
- ediati (the why)
- ekataba (the fall)
- eparthenoi (the conceit of apparent purity)
- demosia (the public acclaim that causes public figures to inflate their egos)
- paidiske (maiden, female slave - seductive aspect)
- eaeidelos (unseen, dark)

RITUAL

On the ground will be the Lilin Society's sigil of Choronzon. The sorcerer should sit on the spiral in the center.

The sorcerer should be have their feet together with the wand held upright with both hands against the body. For a little while be in complete silence and empty your mind. Then the wand should be held sideways above the head. All the while he will stare into a tetrahedron crystal. He will focus on the crystal as he begins this chant. The chant should be done in a loud and firm manner, one that demands rather than asks.

"ANETAB OTHIL LUDSI CAOSAGI
ZIRDO LONSMI DEPEDE ZARZAX

SOBA DOOAIN MAD ZILODARPE
TOOAT GMICALZOMA LARSAD TOLGLO
YPROIL LATOK OVCHO ASYMP
UNCHI OMORS ZODACARE GOHUS
OADRIAK OROCHA DOPAL CAOSAGI
ABRAMAG NETAAIB CAOSAGI IO CHORONZON"

Visualize energy coming down from the crystal and striking you. Feel the energy in your body as it vibrates throughout. Slam the wand on the ground. and shout "CHORONZON"

Now meditate and focus on the abyss. Imagine it as total darkness. Imagine yourself confronting the abyss and crossing it. Imagine it consuming your ego. Let Choronzon rot away the Demiurge's curse and let him awaken the inner Azoth (spirit).

Images of fear, death and absolute horror will overcome the mind of the sorcerer at first, but as you continue you will accept these images and the feelings of insecurity will be replaced with one of bliss as you become one with nothingness.

When all visions and sensations fade write everything in your journal. That night you may have a message in the form of a dream. Take great care to write it down in the morning.

GNOSIS OF LILITH-SOPHIA

The universe began with the original unknown god who has been referred to as Bythos. He emanated further aeons in pairs of lesser beings. These beings form the acausal beings as we known them. The world was lawless chaos and infinite, as was meant to be. The formless becoming form was a flaw.

It was Sophia who brought about this flaw, by "birthing" the Demiurge who brought about creation of materiality. After falling from the unknown god she feared that she would be destroyed. She was confused and longed to return to the unknown god and it's these desires to return to the unknown god which led to the creation of the Demiurge. The Demiurge is ignorant of Sophia yet still manages to infuse the spiritual sparks into his creation.

Sophia is wisdom, further more she is wisdom to bring change in the spirit. She is gnosis. She is Lilith and Hecate and thus the source of individual power and gnosis. We now see that if Lilith is Sophia than it is Lilith who brought forth the Demiurge. She was unaware of the nefarious intentions of her "child" and has since tried to bring back the stolen spirits to the primordial darkness where they belong.

Since the acausal beings are amoral, she has no problem with destroying her "child". He is the deceitful ruler of this world which stands in opposition to everything Sophia represents. In the Garden of Eden she grew a tree in hope that mankind would find it, in the form of an apple. She and her and Satan together invaded the Demiurge's "paradise" guised as a serpent.

RITUAL

The sigil of Lilith-Sophia will be drawn on the ground.

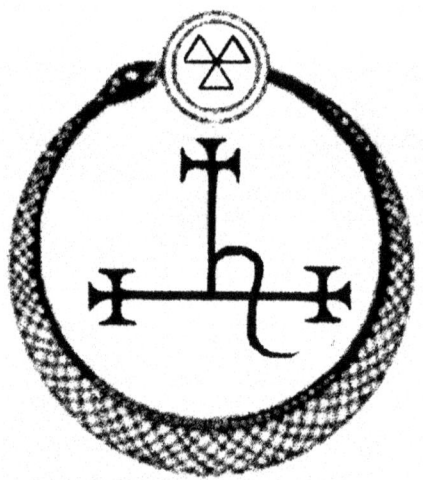

The sorcerer will stand in the center of this sigil. At each direction (north, south, east and west) place a black candle and light it. With the athame pointed in each direction while facing that direction recite the following.

Facing South: "By the forces of Hell and the Wrathful Gods I call upon Lucifer, the adversary of Archangel Michael"

Facing West: "By the forces of Hell and the Wrathful Gods I call upon Leviathan, the adversary of Archangel Gabriel."

Facing East: "By the forces of Hell and the Wrathful Gods I call upon Asmodeusu, the adversary of Archangel Raphael."

Facing North: "By the forces of Hell and the Wrathful Gods I call upon Belial, the adversary of Archangel Uriel"

Now while holding the athame out while turning counterclockwise recite three times "Veni omnipotens aeterne diablus"

Chant "so-phi-a" starting low and deep and gradually getting louder and higher pitched until you are shouting. Then raise your left hand and slice it open, spilling the blood on the sigil.

"Lilith-Sophia, I call to you. Hear my words as I ask you to grant me knowledge, knowledge which has been forbidden by your creation. I ask that you channel down through this nexion I call my body. Great and powerful bride of Satan, Lilith-Sophia, I spill my own blood to feed you. Accept my sacrifice and bring me knowledge.

Now bring in the sacrifice (the sacrifice should be in the circle with you. Never leave the circle during this ritual).

"Lilith-Sophia, I present you with this proper sacrifice. May the blood spilt fuel the your acausal needs and in return leave me with gnosis."

Now meditate while standing. This will prove difficult because your body will constantly irritate and disrupt your concentration through cramps. Ignore them and feel the power of Lilith-Sophia running throughout your body, up your spine and into your head. You will feel a jolt of electricity.

Now step out and write down any visions, words or any feelings during the ritual in your journal. Pay attention to your dreams over the next week, looking for more visions.

A SACRIFICE TO CHORONZON TO BRING DESTRUCTION

Start with the sigil of Choronzon on your altar. In the center of the altar is a tetrahedron crystal. Light a black candle to the left and right of the crystal. The sorcerer will develop a circle around the altar and will never leave the circle.

At each direction (north, south, east and west) place a black candle and light it. With the athame pointed in each direction while facing that direction recite the following.

Facing South: "Facing By the forces of Hell and the Wrathful Gods I call upon Lucifer, the adversary of Archangel Michael"

Facing West:"By the forces of Hell and the Wrathful Gods I call upon Leviathan, the adversary of Archangel Gabriel."

Facing East: "By the forces of Hell and the Wrathful Gods I call upon Asmodeusu, the adversary of Archangel Raphael."

Facing North: "By the forces of Hell and the Wrathful Gods I call upon Belial, the adversary of Archangel Uriel"

Now while holding the athame out while turning counterclockwise recite three times "Veni omnipotens aeterne diablus"

Chant "Cho-ron-zon" while gazing deep in the crystal. Keep a low and deep tone. Let the chant echo throughout your being. Picture the abyss in the crystal, its whirling storms and chaos.

"Choronzon, I call to you."

Now chant "om" and project it toward the crystal.

"Choronzon, I call to you and ask that you channel chaos into this world. Bring the darkness with you from the abyss and eat away at the fabric of this existence. I now sacrifice blood in your honor."

Now kill your sacrifice and spill the blood onto the crystal. Chant "Cho-ron-zon" while gazing into the ritual.

Choronzon may react in many ways from causing insanity in a human to kill others in large numbers or causing massive earthquakes. Pay attention to the news for the next week and look for signs that your ritual worked. Sometimes you may have a prophetic dream of what is to come

LILIN SOCIETY CREED

I accept Satan as my god but bow to no god. I find in his word absolute lawlessness and thus shall personify this upon this Earth.

I believe there exists life beyond the forms. This world is an illusion.

I shall not fear death. I shall bring death if needed. I shall end my own life if it empowers this movement of Satanism.

I will work to strengthen the sinister, always keeping goals in mind, never to lose sight.

I reject the weak, the botched and the spiritually sick. This is the mundane and they are my enemy.

I believe in brotherhood. I will support my brothers and sisters no matter what.

I shall live amoral and decide for myself what is acceptable.

Because I know there is life after the death of this body I feel no pity ending a life. I am prepared to spill blood when blood needs spilling.

Chaos is the beginning and so shall it be the end.

Hail Satan, Lord of Chaos, Lord of Sitra Achra. Bring me honor or bring me death.

RITUAL TO LEVIATHAN TO BRING DESTRUCTION

Leviathan: the abysmal serpent, Ruler of the waters of Chaos and the Embodiment of annihilation.

Leviathan is the acausal essence beyond the mundane forms. He is in opposition to order. He is the omnipresent bringer of darkness and sinister. He rules the waters of chaos that will flood the cosmic order, drowning all creation in its molten lava.

He is called upon to manifest the chaos and sinister into the causal world. He can create mass hysteria and cause humans to commit desperate and violent acts.

He is essential in all rituals with the aim to bring about evolution in the spirit of man through internal and external sorceries. If called upon in aeonic workings his influence will be like a black cloud of pestilence plaguing the planet. He gives the sorcerer what it takes to overcome his obstacles in this causal world.

RITUAL

This ritual is conducted at a shore line. Start by facing the water. This should be done at night on an empty beach. With your wand trace the esoteric sigil of the nexion. Envision it fusing with your body. Now draw the esoteric sigil of chaos. Combine the two sigils, one burning red and one burning blue until they form a new color.

Draw the sigil of Leviathan now in the center and shout toward the ocean. "In the name of chaos, in the name of lawlessness, in the name of Satan, in the name of Leviathan. He who dwells in the primordial ocean, who rules its depths, who aims to drown creation; I _____ invite you to this world to wage chaos."

"In the name of the Chavajoth, and the acausal bridge, Qayin, I ask that you cross this bridge and through my nexion unleash your magnificent power."
"In the name of nothingness, in the name of the origin, in the name of the unknown god, I call you forth, Leviathan. Bring with you a tsunami of chaos and let its wrath be felt throughout the planet. Shake it at its core and without mercy let the profane perish."

"In the name of the Chavajoth I come to you on my knees and ask that you open the gate to the other side, Sitra Achra, and bring death and pestilence to this planet. Let the blood boil and skin melt free so the Azoth can be free. Let us release through your cleansing and boiling water."

"Satan, Lilith, Qayin, Luluwa, Chavajoth, Leviathan" repeat this eleven times. Now step into the water and raise your hands to the sky and recite a mantra. Meditate on the moon.

SATANIC ALCHEMY OF THE BEING

Physical Alchemy: Here is where the neophyte initiates into the sinister way. Here you will train the ego to forsake all the mundane world has forced upon you. You will train it to welcome the darkness. This is the first step toward evolution. This involves partaking in sinister acts through sorcery as well as practical means. Do not limit yourself, awaken your inner darkness.

Astral: Here you will further the development of your new ego by detaching yourself from emotion. You will develop further your misanthropy and lose all signs of empathy for mundanes. You will learn to no longer relate to them for you have truly began the path of the sinister.

Mental: Here you will evolve your mind to think beyond science, beyond all that the world has taught you. You will practice and master self control as well as stillness of the mind. You will master focusing with your mind and ignoring your body. You will develop manipulation of the mundane world to further the Satanic movement.

Spiritual: You will, through your dark ego, access your Azoth (spirit) and open the long closed nexion gates to the acausal. You will begin to understand chaos and use it in your art.

Completion: You will open your third eye and let acausal flow throughout your mind, spirit and body. You will bring chaos into the acausal world through the nexion which is your mind and body. You will shed causal anchors of this world. Your hatred will further fuel you. This is your step toward immortality.

REACHING THE LILITH QLIPHA

Here is the dark side of the astral worlds. This is where nightmares manifest into prophecy. This is as far as the Sorcerer can progress on the Tree of Death without dying, for here Lilith is the arachnid that weaves death into the causal world.

To reach this qlipha one must draw Lilith's sigil on the ground and sit in it. Bring anything you need with you into the sigil because here you will remain until the ritual is complete. Because of the dangers of this ritual, only adepts are to use it.

Start with an invocation of Lilith. Surround yourself with black and red candles around the sigil. Begin breathing techniques and when you have stilled your body chant her name low. Stare into a tetrahedron crystal which should be at eye level.

"Lilith of the dark acausal world, Lilith the nurturing mother, Lilith weaver of death, arachnid mother, Lilith-Sophia, I call to you from this world to come to me and enter this nexion. I invoke you, chaotic spirit."

Now kill your sacrifice and spill the blood on the crystal.

"Lilith I call to you. Invoke me."

Now meditate. Get yourself in a waking dream state for this sphere is concerned with dreams. No matter how horrible the images are remain with it until completion.

When you are done thank Lilith and write down everything you saw, heard and felt in a journal. Due to the possibility of seizures (which Lilith is known to give) take great caution, especially with the candles around you.

THE CHAVAJOTH

Satan: Ruler of Sitra Achra, Lord of darkness, return me to the origin.

Moloch: Guardian of the flames that cleanse the spirit. Cast me in your fires so that I may know myself and understand the lawless chaos.

Beelzebuth: Lord of Flies let my body decay along with my ego.

Lucifuge Rofocale: He who flees the light, he from the shadows let me become engulfed with the darkness.

Astaroth: Sadistic king of murder, let me feel the death. Cruel sadist I am your masochist.

Asmodeus: God of Vengeance, let my enemies perish in your wrath.

Belphegor: Lord of dead bodies, I deliver this useless corpse in your honor. Free me of this flesh.

Baal: Mighty God of War let your wrath of battle fill the planet through aeonic sorcery.

Adramelek: the Ruler of Deception, allow me to infiltrate undetected so that I may bring chaos to the causal.

Lilith: Dark Queen and Princess of Chaos, let me understand. Open my mind the the acausal.

Naamah: Mistress of sexuality, I submit to you and all the pleasures you offer.

PRAYER OF THE DARK CROSSROADS
Where our worlds intersect
I see you standing at that tree

Its long dead limbs hang lifeless
dark figure in shadows hide
father of the darkest mysteries
conduit of my sorcery
Kalfu, by chaos I'm bound
Kalfu, I wait at the crossroads

OMOLU PRAYER
Bones and rotting skin
graveyard dusk and corpse musk
Omolu of Calunga
do you hear me?
Omolu, Lord of Death
do you hear me?

PRAYER TO CHONRONZON
where one world ends one begins
a fusion of both energies
demon of anti-matter
all dissolving, decaying
Choronzon, I call to you
Choronzon of the abyss
aid me in my ascension
lift me beyond the veil

THE TEN HELLS IN SEVEN PLACES

The following is an expansion on the work of Aleister Crowley to give more dept. I have noted the expansions in italic.

1 Kether, 2 Chokmah, 3 Binah: שאול Sheol (Grave)
This is the final resting place of the body, the form the creator had given us when he stole the sparks. This is thus where rebirth begins.
"And nail my coffin shut."

4 Chesed: אבדון Abaddon (Perdition)
This is the place of the bottomless pit. It rest in agony beside שאול, *the realm of the dead. King of the locusts, Ἀβαδδών. The destroyer.*
"Bring destruction upon this causal existence, Oh great Abaddon! Rejoiced are we to be in the land of the dead."

The grave is naked above him and destruction has no covering.
it is a fire that consumes to abaddon
shall thy loving kindness be declared in the grave or thy faithfulness in abaddon
"Bring destruction, great abaddon!"
Hell and Abaddon are never full; so the eyes of man never satisfied.
torrents of Belial burst into abdaddon
One of many compartments to abaddon.
Great and powerful angel of the abyss, king of the plague of locusts.

5 Geburah: בארשחת Bar Shachath (Clay of Death)
This is the clay that the Demiurge trapped us in. By alchemy of the spirit we can transform the ego. Darken the ego.
"Shatter the clay and free my spirit."
From the earth our bodies came, to the earth shall they return but our spirit is chaos and chaos can never die.

6 Tiphareth: טיטהיון Titahion (Pit of Destruction)
This is where the clay shall be destroyed by the hammers of the gods.
"Strike with all your might."
But thou shalt bring them down into the pit of destruction: bloody and deceitful men shall not live out half their days.

7 Netzach: שערימות Shaarimoth (Gates of Death)
This is where we enter the phase between rebirths. Recall the fetus in the umbilical cord noose. Where there is decay there is eternal life
"Return me to origin."

8 Hod: אלמות Tzelmoth (Shadow of Death)
Deep darkness, where light dares not to shine.
"Only horror to the profane but beauty to the fire born."

9 Yesod, 10 Malkuth: גיהנם Gehinnom (Hell)
The burning flames which cleanse man of their mortality
"Gods of Hell, I accept thee."

THE COSMIC HOLOCAUST
1. Listen closely for the profane live amongst you. They hide in the light and avoid the darkness. They praise the cosmic tyrant, the worthless creator of physical existence. Listen closely to the word.
2. And behold, the children of my children's blood burns.
3. And behold, the children of Adam are void of spirit.

4. And behold, the time draws near where we all must awaken and choose a side. Those whom side with the Demiurge shall be punished for they have deserted all that is natural and free. Only destruction can free these slaves.
5. And to their temples set fire, desecrate their houses of worship and act upon them with hate, my children of Qayin.
6. And those with spirit will feel the dissidence in their blood. The clayborn know only one thing, and that is servitude. They cannot know the dissidence, nor can they comprehend defying the law of the cosmic creator.
7. Do you feel the blood in your veins burn? Do you feel the dissidence inside of you. Then you are fireborn and certainly of spirit.
8. Crush the skulls of the weak sheep of the creator. Bash in their heads and slice open their bellies. Carve out their eyes and hack out their tongues. Burn the scripture of lies and deceit.
9. And the slaves to the creator have taken his logic and law and fashioned it upon Earth. Crush these forms and let only chaos rule.
10. And as the end nears we will see uproar among the creator's slaves. They will lash out at each other with claims that their way is right. The war begins in the East and ends in the West. A great fire carried by the desert sands.
11. And when the twins were fed to Moloch, this started the beginning of the end. Cosmic order elasticity has begun to deadline. A great holocaust will spread throughout the cosmos. An inferno in which all will be dissolved.
12. And in the end the spirits will be free, free from the bondage of their clayform. They will join the rest in chaos. And as the Demiurge dies, so shall creation.

AN HONOR TO BELIAL

Being a virgo I have a strong connection with Belial. This is the demon I have devoted myself to and thus have built this ritual to honor the demon.

In the Dead sea scrolls Belial is the leader of the Sons of Darkness.

"You *11* made Belial for the pit, angel of enmity; in darkness is his domain, his counsel is to bring about wickedness and guilt. All the spirits *12* of his lot are angels of destruction, they walk in the laws of darkness; towards it goes their only desire."

Belial's number is one, one being the number that represents earth and remaining firm to one's convictions.

Belial's color is black, black being the color of the primordial chaos before the Earth.

Belial's element is Earth, Earth being the element that sustains humanity.

Belial's direction is north, north being the representation of constantly striving forward and upward toward a Satanic Dawn.

Belial's human element is remaining firm to one's own beliefs. Find out for yourself what is acceptable and stick with it.

Belial's altar element is the incense coal, representing Earth and mankind holding the flame of Lucifer.

Belial's highest manifestation is through understanding and living the natural laws of our carnal self. Indulge and by indulging honor Belial.

This ritual is conducted after a three day fast. During this fast you will sleep no more than three hours a night and eat only at 3:00 a.m. Eat only the minimum to survive.

On the day of the undertaking bring in your sacrifice. Draw the sigil of Belial on the floor and set up an altar in the center of the sigil. Wear a pendant of Belial. On the altar one should have the sigil of Belial painted red on a black painted wood.

Begin with a prayer to Satan.

"In the name of the anti cosmic father, bringer of chaos, I call to you. I honor thee in my sinister path and strengthen the current to dismantle the cosmic. Hail Satan."

Now burn coal in a pot. Let the aroma fill the room. Light one black candle and place it to the left of the Belial sigil. At the base of the sigil place graveyard dirt.

"Great Belial, leader of the Sons of Darkness, carnal demon of the primordial black, I call to you to honor you. Accept this ritual and my devotion to you."

Meditate while chanting Belial's name. This should remain low and projected forward toward the sigil. Close your eyes and visualize the sigil taking a life of its own as it grows and shrinks. Take notice of any other visions that come to mind.

Now shout

"In the name of Belial I sacrifice for you. Feed off the blood and accept this gift."

Now slit the throat of your sacrifice. Spill the blood onto the altar, focusing on the sigil.

RITUAL TO TANIN'IVER

Tanin'Iver is said to be the mechanism of evil and relates to the copulation between Satan and Lilith. If Satan and Lilith were to have a child together it would be the death of the planet, causal beings to bring about the sinister. Because they are spiritual and without form they must steal the souls of humans to spread their chaos.

If this sexual act were to come forth, Tanin'Iver, the blind dragon, will commit to the process. Satan and Lilith must copulate within the presence of the blind dragon.

Fire is the key to give Tanin'Iver his sight again. This blindness must be lifted for he must observe the copulation in order for the wrathful demons to invade creation. The Demiurge has impaired Tanin'Iver's ability, thus hindering the process of creating these anti cosmic beings. He extinguished his flame and blinded him.

When the day comes that Tanin'Iver opens his eyes we will see the union of Satan and Lilith and thus chaos will return to its original form.

This is a ritual to Tanin'Iver

This ritual is conducted while staring into a tetrahedron crystal.

"Tanin'Iver, blind dragon, we empower you and your flame."

"We awaken you and rekindle the flames of Satan"

"Blind Dragon, see again so this world can be demolished."

"Unite Satan and Lilith."

"Mechanism of evil, hear my chant!"

conluent flammis caecorum (This last part is chanted for an undetermined amount of time. Start low and deep and eventually get loud and shrieking as you project it at the crystal.

Formulas
laus Belial
A praise to Belial, can be used in all working with Belial, especially a mantra.

filii tenebrarum triumphantes
Sons of Darkness, Triumphant is a call to the Sons of Darkness led by Belial to defeat the Sons of Light

ecce calicem veneno, Samael

A formula when dealing with rituals pertaining to Gnosis and the "venom of god"

Da mihi bibere, Lilith
A great mantra when working with Lilith

porro triumphator in inferno sunt
A great mantra for any ritual

et revertetur ad tenebras
Another great Mantra

THE HARDSHIPS OF THIS PATH

The infernal path toward enlightenment is hardly a leisure stroll. The road is full of depression and an extreme sense of alienation. I often find myself detached from the rest of humanity the more I see past the illusion. Everything seems futile. Understanding is what will help you get through this.

Depression is a symptom of spiritual evolution. It is the spirit's eye seeing past the ego and understanding that life is an unfulfilling void of distractions until death. This is why Satanists will more often than most harbor suicidal tendencies or idealization; as our understanding grows so does our desire to leave this world.

The main problem with suicide is that the Satanist is not ready to die. He has not fully shed his ego and has not reached the proper state of gnosis. He has too many anchors in this world, and these anchors will drag the Satanist back through the vicious cycle of rebirth with a new ego to start over again. It takes more than one lifetime to fully reach the pinnacle of gnosis and break the cycle of rebirth, thus returning to chaos.

I have grown envious of the incarcerated at times. They have been put in the perfect situation to kill their ego, in seclusion from the distractions of this world. The problem is that many misspend their time with the demiurge cults and mindless criminal activity. Segregation is a path towards enlightenment and thus we get to my suggestion.

I feel that once a week, or once every two weeks, the Satanist should segregate himself from the world. No stimulation, no music, no television, no reading; nothing but his thoughts and mind. During this time the Satanist should fast to weaken the body and strengthen the mind. Learn to ignore your body, learn to ignore your ego.

This will seem futile at first perhaps and the physical world will claw at your brain and try to pull you back in but don't let it. This is a necessary abstinence which in time will help you reach gnosis. Truth be told, rituals exist mainly to satisfy mankind's need for them, but what good are all the rituals when your ego still dominates?

The main problem I have with the modern Satanist is that he is too egotistical and hypocritical. He is self-absorbed in attaching himself to a community he wishes to relate to. On the outside he is rebellious and dominant but inside he strives for attention. He proclaims his devotion to chaos and Satan and then fills his spiritual matters with physical idols and symbols which he seems to worship more than the actual representation of them.

If this is you, and you accept this as being true, than you are finally on the right path. Work within the realm of segregation and get to know your real spirit. You already know your ego.

This path is not an easy one to walk. Enlightenment and evolution comes with hard work but the end payoff is well worth all the sacrifice. You shed blood in your rituals, you chant and you pray. You follow all the orders and steps but what good is it if you don't understand yourself; and by that I mean your true self not you ego.

UNDERSTANDING THE ILLUSION

In the occult community we have heard the phrase a lot. Life is an illusion. In Chao- Gnosticism it is believed the Demiurge has cast a veil over the sparks to trick them as to what reality is. But seldom does anyone break it down to explain it from a scientific level to help the world see how the Demiurge accomplishes this. It all starts when we are a fetus and a little organ called the pineal gland.

The fetus develops the pineal gland at forty nine days after conception. Coincidently the Buddhist believes it takes forty-nine days for the soul to reincarnate. What we know about the pineal gland is that it is the seat of consciousness, a nest of our soul. At first it develops in the mouth of the fetus and makes its way to the brain. So what is so special about this little cone shaped organ?

It is the only un-paired part of the brain and it is present in all mammals. It is responsible for producing melatonin and most importantly dimethyltryptamine or DMT. DMT is always produced in the brain and creates a psychedelic experience (DMT can be taken recreationally) that is controlled. This means that the reality we see every day is a controlled psychedelic trip, an illusion or the veil.

Now when we take psychedelic drugs in uncontrolled means we throw the pineal gland off and thus we are presented with chaotic images of what we call a psychedelic trip. LSD, mushrooms, ketamine and even marijuana give us a release from the veil, although temporary and to a lesser degree.

The veil is still there but it is weakened.

To understand this one must understand that cosmic order operates under the laws of science whereas chaos does not. The pineal gland produces the DMT which is a chemical reaction used to nullify and tweaks our perception; to control us. In the physical world we live the veil is only beneficial so we can operate here, to study the occult sciences and strengthen our soul to prevent reincarnation. Once we die the veil is lifted, for our consciousness is free from the clay prison and the control of the demiurge UNLESS he re traps you and reincarnates you. Those who have devoted their lives to Satan and death will be the lucky ones who get the chance to return to origin, cosmic chaos.

PRAISE TO TUBAL CAIN

Tubal-Cain is the descendent of Qayin, son of Lamech and Zillah and brother to Naamah. He was a master forger of all weapons made of bronze and iron. He is thus a master of war and is regarded as such in our tradition.

We honor him with the following ritual.

If you have the skill form an excellent blade from iron. If not then simply acquire one, however it must be made with superior craftsmanship.

Light a fire in a metal bowl. Take a sacrifice and slice its throat, making sure blood is on the blade. Place the blade in the flames.

"Great Tubal-Cain, I give you praise. I honor you with blood from an iron weapon. I thank you for crafting weapons made to slay the profane. In the name of Satan, all hails."

THE SEXUAL RITES OF NAAMAH

Naamah is the first you encounter in your ascent on the tree of death. It's the first face of the faceless queen, Lilith, and requires absolute submission. One gives into their carnal nature when dealing with Naamah as she takes the dominant role. This is true for both male and female.

A pendant is made the day prior to the ritual. It is a glass vial filled with semen and menstrual blood. It is blessed by Lilith in the following manner.

Face south and place the vial into a pomegranate. Burn sulfur and cinnamon. Place in the pomegranate a moonstone.

"Lilith, I ask that you bless this sexual elixir."

Now meditate, focusing on the sigil of Lilith.

The next day you take the vial and wear it around your neck. You will be naked except for this pendant.

Stand and face the south and chant Naamah's name, projecting it South.

"Naamah, great demon of prostitution, ruler of Nehemoth, I call to you to honor you. I offer myself in carnal ecstasy before your human bone throne. By the powers of the Chavajoth, I call to you."

Now kneel and get into a deep meditated state. Visualize Naamah in all her beauty. Her corpse pale skin, her voluptuous breasts, the curves which stress her femininity.

Envision the two of you suspended in dusk. All around you is endless night without form. The two of you hang in the night with your bodies wrapped tight. Imagine the act of intercourse and imagine the beauty and power of the act, not simply as a means to carnal desire but as an act of sorcery.

Be detailed in your vision. When you climax whisper.

"My devotion to you, Naamah."

For up to a week the night queen will visit you in dreams. Welcome her and pay attention to the dream for signs and messages.

PART FOUR: FROM INITIATE TO ADEPT

INTRODUCTION

In tradition of the Lilin Society an adept is one who has proven his skills. Anyone can claim adeptship, but those that truly have earned this rank will reap the rewards. In our tradition adeptship is earned over a period of time. It is impossible to put a timeframe on such a task for each initiate is different.

Different sects, temples, societies etc have constructed their own battery of tests to accomplish this, and we have done the same. The core goal of the Lilin Society has always been an evolution of the individual. This is achieved through both practical and esoteric praxis. If we were to have a motto it would be "insight through suffering".

What separates us from the many other groups operating out there is that our focus on practical means is just as vital as those of esoteric. The practical means include physical texts, physical pain management, insight roles etc. We have developed the following program which will aid in the discovery of the hidden adept. After achieving adeptship you can further your ascension towards evolution and beyond.

INITIATION RITUAL

Adeptship starts with this simple yet extremely powerful ritual. The initiate is like a newborn infant. He must learn to crawl, walk and finally run toward his evolution. In this stage the initiate, regardless of past accomplishments, will acknowledge in this tradition that he truly is at the start of his quest toward self evolution.

The ritual is conducted outside near a river. It is conducted during the hour of Saturn. The initiate will bring with him a tetrahedron crystal, a journal, and a black robe. Underneath the robe he is to be naked.

Let the moonlight shine upon you and raise the crystal to it. Envision the lunar sorcery of Lilith shining down and empowering the crystal.

"Who I once was means little, who I will become is what matters. Through pain, suffering and adversity I will learn the steps toward my personal evolution. All weakness is now forgotten, all hidden strength awoken, and today I declare my initiation toward adeptship."

Now place the crystal on a log, rock etc and kneel in front of it. Meditate and as you do this search for your personal sigil. Once you discover it immediately draw it. No one is ever to see this sigil. You must carry it with you the entire time during this path toward adeptship.

Now remove your robe and step into the river until it comes waist high. Raise your hands to the sky and shout to the moon "Hail Satan".

INVOKING THE SPIRIT OF QAYIN

Starting on this path your goal should be to personify the dark lord, Satan. Before this one must personify the first Satanist, Qayin. Much like Qayin you must learn your path through the pains and adversities and awaken the black flame within.

This ritual is conducted during the hour of Saturn. Draw the esoteric sigil of Qayin upon the ground (note: This sigil is developed after meditation prior to this ritual. Focus on Qayin until a sigil comes to mind.) Step into the center of the circle. Spread broken glass onto the ground and kneel down on your bare knees onto the glass. Put pressure on your knees to cut them so you bleed and activate the sigil. Focus on the pain. Now take a knife and cut your left arm three times; once for Satan, once for Lilith and once for Qayin. Hold your left arm up and bleed onto the sigil.

"Master Qayin, first murderer and Satanist, I call to you. Aid me on my path toward adeptship. Give me the power to overcome my weakness and obstacles. In the name of the almighty Satan I invoke your spirit, Qayin."

Now pour salt in the wounds on your arm. Do not scream. Take the pain and fight through it and focus on it, turning it into energy. Store this energy.

Now stand and walk out of the room. Take a shower and imagine all weakness leaving your body as the spirit of Qayin empowers you.

THE INFERNO PATH

The Inferno Path has been designed to break you down and rebuild you strong. On this path you will endure physical, emotional and mental stress. If you fail any section of this test you must start the initiation process over again when you are more prepared for it. If you feel the need you can conduct the tests described as many times necessary.

The first thing we will discuss is strength training. These physical exercises are conducted every day during your quest down the path. Before we discuss the exercise routine let's explain a couple of the exercises.

Pyramids: These are done in sets. We start at the bottom of a pyramid and work our way up. Taking pushups for example, we would do ten pushups, rest, then nine, rest, then eight etc until you reach one. Once you reach one you must now come down the pyramid starting at one and working your way to ten.

30-60's: This is thirty seconds of sprinting and sixty seconds of walking.

You will alternate every day the four exercise schedules described. When you reach day five you simply start over again. If you cannot complete an exercise day just push yourself until you can't handle any more. Push yourself to the limits.

Exercise One: Pushup pyramids, crunch pyramids, 30-60's (x5), three mile hike carrying fifty pounds, pushup pyramids, crunch pyramids, 1 mile run.

Exercise Two: Pushup pyramids, crunch pyramids, 30-60's (x3), three mile run, pushup pyramids, crunch pyramids

Exercise Three: Pushup pyramids, crunch pyramids, five mile run, pushup pyramids, crunch pyramids

Exercise four:1 mile run, 30-60's (x5), five mile hike carrying fifty pounds.

Always end all exercise sections with a half hour meditation.

THE MORAL TEST

A Satanist is amoral in that morals are subjective and thus it is up to the individual to decide for themselves what is acceptable behavior. In this test you will act in a sinister way. You'll conduct yourself as the adversary to moral norms. You will deliberately shatter people with your words and actions. This test is to give insight as to whether a moral is true to the individual, or just one instilled upon you by causal abstraction. This test will last one week.

INSIGHT ROLE

I will not go deep into insight roles here, I discuss them in various MSS (i.e. Aeon of Sinister Empathy, Manual of the Drecc). Basically an insight role is one you take that is at odds with your nature to experience insight and evolution of yourself. An example would be a Satanist becoming a hardcore Christian. The role is a sudden change in behavior and people need to believe it. This role lasts for a period of time and when it is over you return to your normal life (unless you are a LS Drecc and living extended insight roles).

Here is a list to give you some ideas…

1. The hardcore Christian: Praise Jesus Christ, fight abortion, bash gay marriage try to convert someone to Christianity.
2. Neo Nazi: Take on Christian Identity as a religion, participate in hate crimes, rally in public and run a national socialist website. Maybe contribute literature to a website.
3. Homosexual: This could be quite the challenge for the straight man.
4. Heterosexual: Also challenging for the gay man.

5. Soldier: Learn to kill and strive for the best. Join the good ol' boy crew.
6. Cop: be a strict cop who never cuts someone a break.
7. Drug Addict: get yourself hooked on drugs for a while. Wallow in its misery.
8. Start a Wicca Coven: Here you can exploit young beautiful women while you are at it.
9. Become an Islamic Extremist
10. Fundamentalist Mormon

These are just some ideas. Use one or come up with your own. Sometimes danger should be involved for when there is a real risk of injury or death, one gets more insight into their individual.

This test should last no less than three months.

SPIRITUAL SEGREGATION

Spiritual segregation is when you remove yourself from the world. This is to avoid human contact, avoid causal distractions such as computers, television etc. This is a time for just you, your mind and your studies. Spiritual segregation should be practiced at least once a month for a day or two *minimum*. Suggested is three consecutive days a month.

RITUAL OF INSIGHT

This ritual is conducted once a week while walking the Inferno Path. You will enter your chamber and draw your personal sigil upon the ground. Enter the sigil. Light eleven black candles around you. Take a chalice of water and bless it to Leviathan (recite a prayer to Leviathan) and then drink it. Now cut open a finger on your left hand and pour salt in the wound. Get into a meditation posture and meditate, ignoring the pain you will focus on your sigil while gazing into a tetrahedron crystal. This ritual should last one hour.

MASTER THE ART

While walking the Inferno Path you will practice the art daily. Become proficient in meditation, mantra, visualization, chanting, scrying, spell craft, rituals, invocations, evocations, internal sorcery, external sorcery and aeonic sorcery. Only the individual can decide when they mastered one of these arts. Be honest with yourself because all adepts must eventually face Choronzon and cross the abyss. If you are not a master of your art then you will fail.

ADEPT RITUAL

Once you feel confident in your tests upon the Infernal Path and you have mastered your arts, than you are ready for the adept ritual.

You will go outside and conduct this ritual during the hour of Saturn. You will start a bonfire. You will hold out in front of you the personal sigil you carried the whole time you were on the Inferno Path.

"I have finished the Infernal Path and shed my body, mind and spirit of all weakness. I have found strength. I shall incorporate what I have learned on this path into my daily life. I will exhibit strength in all forms. I am a master of my art, and master of my self. I am now able to personify my dark lord, Satan. I shall walk the sinister path for I have passed my initiation and now have earned the title of adept."

Now toss the sigil into the fire and watch it burn. This is symbolic of the adept passing through the cleansing flames and being reborn with knowledge. Raise your hands to the sky and shout "Hail Satan".

PART FIVE:
RUNNING YOUR OWN SECT

INTRODUCTION

The Lilin Society exists as a means to learn and teach the esoteric dark arts. The goal is spiritual evolution and achieving gnosis. This can be a solitary path (most members choose this path) however it can work in group settings as well. What this book's intentions are is to educate the member on how to create and run your own sect under the Lilin Society umbrella.

Understand that in order to be recognized by the Lilin Society you must adhere by their rules. You can feel free to add to the rules but they cannot be in conflict with those written by Asha'Shedim.

Rituals will be given here but I also encourage you to create your own customs and rituals and even share them with me. I may indoctrinate them into the Lilin Society as a whole (of course giving credit to whoever creates them).

As a Sect of the Lilin Society you will have many enemies. Although violence hasn't come of it I feel obligated to let you know what you will be patched under. After the formation of your sect feel free to contact Asha'Shedim from the Lilin Society website with your accomplishment.

The Satanic Points

These should be taught to every initiate and although not necessary to memorize it would be great if a member does and that member should be recognized for it. These Satanic Points along with the Code of Sinister Honour must be printed in every initiation packet.

1. We believe in the existence of Cosmic Chaos and Cosmic Order.

2. We believe Cosmic Chaos is the infinite origin.

3. We believe Cosmic Order is a finite enslavement.

4. We believe the god of Cosmic Order is a demiurge, a tyrant.

5. We believe in strength and spiritual evolution.

6. We believe our spirit is infinite, thus originates in this Cosmic Chaos, the acausal plane of unmanifested existence.

7. We are practitioners who dedicate our lives and mind to the art.

8. We believe in the unknown god of Chaos. We believe Satan rules Sitra Achra, the adverse of cosmic order. Sitra Achra is not Chaos, but a step toward it.

9. We do not believe in the Christian version of Satan. He was not a fallen angel.

11.We believe life is the illusion and death is the eternity of the soul.

11. We believe in reincarnation but strive to prevent it. We wish to return to Ur-Chaos.

12. We believe in brotherhood. We shall help those within the Society and never turn on a member within the Society. We are bound by spirit, and thus shall aid each other in spiritual matters.

13. We believe in secrecy. We are bound by our oath and shall not discuss secrets with non members.

14. We are Satanists and we believe in blood ritual. Let the prana empower.

15. We are a society. We do not have priests or masters. The only real statue above member is the Council which serves to screen new members and enhance the Society and its direction. No Satanist shall bow before any other Satanists for it puts them in a position of submission. We do not submit.

16. We believe in acausal energy and that humans are nexions to the acausal realm, this explains sorcery.

17 .We believe in three forms of sorcery; Causal, Acausal and Aeonic.

18. We believe in human sacrifice through Sorcery and that is the only means of Human Sacrifice.

19. We believe that all human sacrifices must be chosen, tested and judged and that their death will benefit Satanism.

20. We believe that morals are subjective and Satan is evil. As Satanists we will personify this evil in our daily lives.

21. We do not reconize the plastic Church of Satan or the Church of Set.

22. We explore all forms of the dark arts and use what works for us without restriction.

23. We believe in acausal entities which exist without form and can be known and contacted through dark sorcery.

24. We believe in acausal empathy, which is the sensitivity and awareness of acausal energies as they exist in humans.

25. We believe that we have the ability to participate in and control our own evolution through the acausal.

26. We believe that esoteric knowledge (gnosis) requires both development of our psychic faculties and practical knowledge of the acausal continuum deriving from acausal beings.

27. Satanism is more than a religion, it is a philosophy and a way of life

LILIN SOCIETY SECT RULES

Again, these important rules are to be included in initiation packets and reflect core rules of the Lilin Society. As for the Book of Ahriman, you are encouraged to write your own Book of Ahriman and fill it with rituals and teachings I have written as well as ones personal to the Sect.

1. Never reveal to a mundane anything that is done within the Sect for all done within the Sect is sacred

2. Always respect and aid your brothers and sisters

3. Always work toward expansion and never be content.

4. Never show the Book of Ahriman to non-members.

5. Live by the code of Sinister Honor at all times

6. Do not fear death for death is an illusion.

7. Mundanes are enemies and can be lied to but never lie to a brother or sister.

8. In regards to human sacrifice read and obey the rules.

9. Do not respect pity of weakness

10. Always test your strength physically, mentally and spiritually.

11. Always built to last the ages.

12. Conquest is never done, always strive for more. When we rule this world we will seek out other worlds.

13. Die rather than submit.

14. Do not waste love on those who do not deserve it.

15. Reject all illusion and lies

INITIATE TO ADEPT TESTING

Each Sect within the Lilin Society can come up with their own tests but what consists here is a series of tests recommended to be either followed or incorporated within your own standard testing.

INITIATE TESTING PHASE ONE

Have the Initiate go home that evening and perform a demon invocation ritual. Have them choose their patron demon and devote themselves to it. When they return the next day have them place their hands on the altar and have them cut open their left palm. Pour salt into the wound and keep reminding them that pain is an illusion and life is a lie. Help them to see past the physical, causal world. Finally have them hike in the woods for four hours, build camp, and then spend the night in meditation.

INITIATE TESTING PHASE TWO

Have the initiate fast for three days and get no more than three hours of sleep each night. On the third day they are to stand before their scrying mirror with a Satanic Rosary (can be a standard size rosary or a 108 prayer bead rosary). Perform a demon invocation ritual and continue until you are successful. Have the initiate use this ritual to curse an enemy. If this is not successful restart the whole process no more than a week later but no less than a day later. Tell the initiate that contact with the demon may be subtle at first.

INITIATE TESTING PHASE THREE

The Initiate will go into the woods where they will set up camp and fast for three days with not more than three hours of sleep a day. The initiate will be given a schedule to follow. This schedule will be followed for three days.

6-8 AM

Clean body and meditate

8-11AM

Walk/hike without rest drinking only water during the hike.

11-1PM

Meditate and crystal chant

1-3 PM

Physically exhausting tasks such as digging or moving rocks

3-6PM

Meditate

6-7PM

Reflection of studies

7-9PM

Build a fire, gather firewood, build meditation earth mound

9-12AM

Meditate, concentrate on the stars and the flame

12-1AM

Demon invocation ritual for strength during this test

1-2AM

Meditation/scrying/chakra aligning/ crystal chanting

2-3AM

Cleansing shower

3-6AM

Sleep

On the third day the schedule is the same as it is all other days with the exception of after sunset. Here on the third day the initiate will reflect, meditate, scry, crystal chant, align chakras until the hour of Saturn. When the hour of Saturn arrives the initiate will stop and perform a pact to Lucifer. He will then cut his hand and hold salt in his hand while chanting Chaos. During the chant the initiate will be looking into a crystal. After this sleep until dawn and the testing is over.

THE BYLAWS

These Bylaws will be included in every initiation packet and once initiation is completed they will be repeated word for word by the initiate. They may be read from the Book of Ahriman for this initiate will soon become an adept.

1. I will devote myself to my practice.

2. The members of this Society are my brothers, they are my sisters. I will aid my brethren in spiritual matters when the time arrives. I will aid in any other way if possible. We are united under this Society.

3. I will never turn on my brother. I will protect my brother and never testify against my brother in a court of law.

4. If a traitor is discovered in our Society I will bring its attention to the Council, even if that member is a friend. An enemy of the Society is an enemy of mine.

5. My brother or sister's enemy is my enemy. I will use the practice to curse his existence all those who wrong my brethren.

6. I will keep secrets secret. I will not breach this by publicly posting secret material. I will take secrets to the grave, even if I decide to one day leave the Society.

7. I will not bring unwanted attention to the Society. I will not commit a crime of any kind in the name of the Society. I have free will and act on free will.

8. I will work toward ascending power spiritually, mentally and physically. I am a Satanist and thus I am not weak by nature.

9. If I have a problem that needs to be addressed within the Society I will bring it before the Council. I will not act on my own against another brethren or Sect that falls under this Society.

10. If I elect to join a Sect under this Society I will remember that the Sect serves under the Lilin Society name and thus the laws of my Sect cannot override the laws of the Society.

11. If I vouch for a member I will take responsibility to introduce them, to inform them. I will use my best judgment when allowing others into this Society.

12. I will work within this Society to spiritually evolve. I will help my brethren evolve. I will help my Society evolve.

13. No fee should ever be forced upon members of this Society. It is not about making money or any other materialistic agenda. We are here for spiritual reasons. Fees can be taken to pay for patches etc, at cost value only.

14. I devote myself to Lord Satan, to the Unknown God, to the Chavajoth. The Demiurge and all his cults are my enemy. I will never forget this.

15. I understand that I can leave the Society at any time. I am not bound here. If operating a Sect within the Society I can remove it from the Society at any time and still it will exist.

16. I will not talk to news media about the Society without the permission of the Grand Council. I will never speak on behalf of the Society, just on my behalf and on the behalf of my Sect.

HISTORY OF THE LILIN SOCIETY

It is important to understand the history of this Society.

The history of the Lilin Society dates back as far as 2005. Asha'Shedim(AKA John Putignano and Aka Paimon) had lived in East Providence Rhode Island. Having been a solitary practitioner for many years. Having grown tired of the weekend Satanists and fake occultists Asha'Shedim formed the Church of Luciferian Light. It existed for a short time, the name alone attracting the exact people he wanted to separate himself from. Not long after he ended the Church of Luciferian Light.

A few months later the Sect of Angra Mainyu was formed. It had much stricter guidelines for joining. A council was formed. The book followed by the Sect was called "The Tome of Ahriman". Asha'Shedim made most of the contribution to this book. He also wrote books released for public, most notably were "Liber Sitra Ahra" and "The Zomiel".

In 2007 there was a falling out between Asha'Shedim and the council. The disagreement could not be resolved and thus the Sect of Angra Mainyu ended with many members forming the Temple of the Weaver. Asha'Shedim returned to solitary practice.

In May 2013 Asha'Shedim returned to form what is now known as the Lilin Society. To prevent a falling out like with the Sect of Angra Mainyu he had divided the Society into various Sects all with a main focus on many occult studies.

STRUCTURE

Each sect should be watched over by a Master, Mistress or both. It is ideal to have both to be fully functional. The Master and Mistress are above the council. Although they have the power to override a council decision it is encouraged to only use this power in extreme situations and in instances when the council forgets the laws it swore to abide by. If ever a council becomes corrupt and things cannot be resolved the Sect is disbanded and a new one is made. The master and mistress lead all ceremonial rituals. They also have the power to initiate people on merit.

The council consists of at least two adepts chosen by the master and mistress. They accept initiates and work with them through the adepts. The council is a democracy in which votes are taken in regards to the Sect. No vote is taken without the master and or mistress present.

The adepts have proven themselves to the council and are responsible for choosing initiates. Initiates are where it all begins. They will be tested for a minimum of four sessions before the council can vote them to adept. An initiate can come up for vote three times. If after three votes they are not promoted to adept they are released from the Sect.

Each sect will have a chamber devoted to ceremony. If this is outside the book of Ahriman is kept at the house of the master or mistress. Each adept may possess a copy of the Book of Ahriman.

Other important roles for adept would be treasurer, teachers, chief of propaganda, scribe, sect historian, record keeper etc. Look to militia layouts for more slots that may need to be filled.

CORE BELIEFS OF THE LILIN SOCIETY

This section must be included in all initiation packets.

With so many definitions and a diverse world of beliefs, this word has become saturated. Anton LaVey exploited it with his mindless hedonistic cult void of a spiritualism while the Temple of Set, although acknowledged a spiritual Satan, aimed at making Satan a family friendly entity.

The Lilin Society takes a Gnostic approach. We do not view Satan as a fallen angel, and reject the Christian concept of Satan. Before I divulge who Satan is let me explain the belief of Chaos Gnosticism.

Outside our cosmos exists an infinite stretch of lawlessness and Chaos. We call this acausal world Ur-Chaos and it interpenetrates all. Here everything is conceivable and it is the womb of the Dragon we call Tiamat. It is the zero dimension which surrounds the essence of the Unknown God.

Like was said, all is possible in Chaos, even the formation of Order. The Demiurge (Yahweh) is a lesser god who formed the Cosmic Order. The Demiurgic Light came down and formed the Tzimtzum, a concept of contraction and condensation which forced the Demiurgic Light down into the Void. The Tzimtzum was the cause of time, space and causality and when the Ain Sof came down it formed the ten emanations of the Demiurge until Malkuth (physical existence).

When this happened the Ain Sof had a second, adverse emanation the formed. This is because of the new found law of cause and effect. Where the finite and cosmic exists, so shall the infinite and anti-cosmic. This adverse to the Sephiroth is called the Qliphoth. Two trees formed; the Tree of Life (Sepfriotic Bondadge) and the Tree of Dead (Qliphotic Liberation). This is also known as Dayside and Nightside. The Nightside we call Sitra Achra had become the antithesis of Cosmic Order.

The purpose of this Sitra Achra is to seep and intrude into Dayside to help in the return of the divine sparks (Azoth) which have been trapped in Clayform (human form), back to the limitless chaos. It is important to know that Sitra Achra was not the left overs of creation, but a formation made according to the newfound laws of the Cosmic. The goal of the "demons" of Sitra Achra are to free the Azoth from their Cosmic prison.

Lucifer or Satan is a part of the Chavajoth, who is the bringer of Black Light (Atazhoth). The Demiurge has blinded mankind with his Demiurgic Light and Satan will bring the truth to help us see again.

Those who seek the unmanifested will be illuminated by Black Light. Those void of the essence of Sitra Achra will not understand it. Lucifer, the bringer of light, will bring the Black Light but it will always be darkness in the eyes of the blind.

Lucifer's light is Gnosis (knowledge) that is the gate to Sitra Achra. In Sitra Achra are the paths to Ur-Chaos, beyond the Crown of Satan. What is Satan's goals? He is here to destroy the cosmic order, the emanations and the Demiurge and to return all to Chaos, including himself whereas the Demiurge seeks to separate. Satan is the liberator who wishes to unite all back to Ur-Chaos. I ask then, who is the real enemy here; Satan or the Great Cosmic Warden?

Before Satan are three dark veils. These emanated from Cosmic Chaos before the formation of the Tree of Death. These Veils are Tohu, Bohu and Chasek. These veils are what made way the Black Light from the outer darkness and into Sitra Achra.

At the throne sits Satan and Moloch. Satan looks up to Chaos while Moloch looks down at the Tree of Death. When Ascending the Tree of Death the final phase of Adeptship comes from passing through the Flames of Moloch. Only after this will the Adept confront Satan.

It is important to know at this point that Satan is not the Unknown God, but he is our way to the Unknown God and thus he is our master. It must be understood that the ancient gods are nameless. The names we give to their essence are just that, names, but they are names that fit them as we get to know them. Other names for Satan include Apep, Angra Mainyu, Ahriman, Set, Samael and many more. He is the adversary to the Demiurge.

The Chavajoth are the eleven anti-cosmic gods which will destroy cosmic order. Chavajoth is the name of the Demiurge in reverse (HVHI) and their names are Beelzebuth, Lucifuge Rofocale, Astaroth, Asmodeus, Belfegor, Baal, Adramelech, Lilith, Naamah, Moloch and Satan. The Chavajoth is described as a sleeping dragon and is the cumulative forces of Sitra Achra/Nightside.

Now we must understand the acasual universe. A living being is able to change, grow and move without any external forces being applied. The force is internal unlike that of ordinary physical matter in the universe like stars, rocks, galaxies or chemical interacting with chemical. This leads us to believe there is a force within us that is not of this cosmos. This is the Azoth and the acasual spirit must descend from an acasual realm.

This is interesting for it points us to acknowledge the fact that every human being is a nexion (gateway) to the acasual realm which cannot be explained in current mathematical equations. It is indescribable by three dimensions and one linear time dimension. In short, this is Chaos. This also explains our ability to use sorcery and other methods unnatural or "supernatural" in this cosmic order. We are a nexion, and thus we have the ability to pull forth from the acasual world and manipulate that around us in the physical.

CONSECRATING THE SACRED TOOLS

The sacred tools are not to be used before reaching External Adept with the exception of the Sacrificial Obsidian Blade. This item is necessary prior and all sacrifices are done with this blade. These items must be consecrated before one can begin the Initiation rituals and tests.

The first tool is the Obsidian Athame. Acquire an obsidian blade and a wooden handle. On the handle carve or burn the sigil of Lucifer and the esoteric sigil of Azoth. During the hour of Saturn light a black candle and hold the blade over the flame. Repeat the phrase

"et aperuerit tibi portas mortis"

Now raise the athame high. Lower it back into the flame.

"In the name of Lord Satan, bringer of the Black Flame and liberator, I consecrate this athame in your name."

Now raise the athame high. Lower it back into the flame and chant "Chaos" ten times slowly. Envision the powers of Sitra Achra charging the tool.

Lift the blade and extinguish the flame. Now take this athame and wrap it in a silk like black fabric and put it away until you reach the Ritual
of the External Adept. Do not look at this blade until the day of ritual and do not reveal it until the ritual begins.

The next tool is the Ceremonial Sigil. The sigil is on the right. This sacred sigil contains the esoteric sigils of Azoth, Acausal energy, Gnosis, Nexion, Abyss and the serpent circle. The sigil should be burnt, carved or painted on a round piece of wood.

Light a black candle with the sigil of Lucifer carved into the side of the candle. Sacrifice an animal and spill the blood over the sigil while chanting "Chaos".

Now recite the consecration prayer substituting the athame for the Ceremonial Sigil. Now place in a silk like black cloth and do not reveal again until the Ritual of the External Adept. If this is to be worn later it must contain 122 black wooden beads.

The next tool is the Serpent Wand. This wand must either be a serpent like wand in that it bends alot like a slithering snake or it must be carved to resemble a snake. Complete the ritual you did to the Ceremonial Sigil and then wrap in the silk like material and do not reveal until the Ritual of the External Adept.

The final tool is the Sacrificial Obsidian Blade. This tool is consecrated exactly like the athame with one exception. It is wrapped in the silk like material for one day and revealed on the hour of Saturn the next day. It is immediately ready for use in all blood shedding.

MEETING OPENING RITUAL

The council will be in back of the altar while the adepts circle the ritual area. Infront of the altar are the master and or mistress. In the center of the circle are the initiates.

Upon the altar are seven black candles, a Baphomet statue, human bones and incense.

Master: We open this meeting with a prayer. (Each member will recite the prayer after each pause.)

Lord Satan, we call you forth, we call to Sitra Achra, Lord Satan bless this room, let your power radiate this chamber, by the chavajoth, by Qayin and Luluwa, by Ama-Lilith, by the unmanifested universe, womb of Tiamat, the unknown god, in the name of Lord Satan so we begin this ritual.

Adepts chant: Sa-tan, Cha-os, Sit-ra, Ach-ra, chav-a-joth The meeting has began.

MEETING CLOSING RITUAL

The participants are in the same places as they were in the opening ritual. Master: Lord Satan, we now close this meeting.

All: Hail Satan

DEVOTION TO SATAN

On the altar are seven black candles. Also have one candle lit at each direction. Face the altar.

"I call forth the great dragons of Sitra Achra. I call forth the wrathful gods of Chavajoth and call forth Lord Satan the adversary. Lord of the raging chaos, acausal spirit at the crown of the Tree of Death, I devote this ritual to you. May my fireborn spirit burn with the black flame" (Recite three times)

Recite a personal prayer written on a piece of paper. Burn the paper on the altar. Meditate while gazing into a scrying mirror.

In closing recite "I thank you Lord Satan. May you leave me with Gnosis. Hail Satan."

FUNERAL RITES OF THE LILIN SOCIETY

The crowd sits as follows. Initiates in the back, Adepts in the middle and Council in the front. All members let out a low chant of an "om". The Master or Mistress enters the room and all goes silent. They stand before the altar.

They lean down and kiss the corpse on the head. He consecrates a circle. This is as follows.

> Earth "Lirach tasa vefa wehlic, Belial"
> Air "Renich tasa uberaca biasa icar, Lucifer"
> Fire "Ganic tasa fubin, Flereous"
> Water "Jedan tasa hoet naca, Leviathan"

After this circle is consecrated

The Master then turns to the crowd.

Master: "_____ served us well. He/she was devoted to the art and their sect. He/she has served Lord Satan well during their time upon their Earth. May their evolved spirit escape rebirth and move forward into the Unmanifested Universe."

"I call upon Euronymous, I call upon Baalberith, I call upon Babael. I call upon these demons to see over this funeral and watch over the departed. Now we will all stand as each row comes up one at a time and places their departing notes into the burning bowl."

Each member beforehand had hand written a personal prayer for the deceased to be watched over. Starting with the Initiates and ending with the Council each member will pass by the body, depositing their note into a large metal bowl.

Now when all are seated the Master will read each note. When he is done he will say "By Flereous your spirit is lifted. In the sacred flames you shall rise." He will then burn the note, dropping it into a separate burning bowl.

The Master now lights incense and waves them over the casket.

Master: "By Lucifer your spirit settles and is released back into the Womb of Tiamat. Hail Chaos."

All: "Hail Satan"

Sand is then poured on the burnt letters.

Master: "By Belial you become one with him. May you find rebirth in Chaos."

A Chalice of consecrated water is poured.

Master: "By Leviathan your spirit is released. May you find rebirth in Chaos."

The sigil of the Patron demon of the deceased is now traced over the bowl with a wand.

Master: "May _____ guide you and watch over you."

Master: "In the name of Lord Satan it is done. We bid farewell to our brother/sister."

Following is a banquet. If there is a living spouse of the deceased they sit at the head of the table.

The Marriage Rites of the Lilin Society

The altar will face the north. The Master or Mistress will begin the ceremony by invoking the elemental circle. This is as follows

Earth "Lirach tasa vefa wehlic, Belial"
Air "Renich tasa uberaca biasa icar, Lucifer"
Fire "Ganic tasa fubin, Flereous"
Water "Jedan tasa hoet naca, Leviathan"
 After this circle is consecrated

The groom waits at the southern portion of the circle as he waits for his bride. Two masked adepts enter the room with the bride and bring her to the groom. The two meet at the southern portion and the adepts walk off. The bride and groom make their way up the center of the circle and stop in the middle. Here they stand for a moment as the center of the circle represents Satan and this is out of respect. The two continue to the altar.

Master or Mistress

"Like Qayin and Luluwa these two burning spirits have found each other They found a love and formed a bond. Rosier gathers us to witness the union of _____ and _____. Before Lord Satan these two wish to remain together as long as they are upon this Earth."
The bride and groom hold hands and the Master or Mistress wraps a red cord around their wrists.

Master or Mistress

"In the name of Satan I bind you to one another."

Participants "Hail Satan"

The bride and groom are now each handed a black candle which they place upon the altar on the left and right of the unity candle, a red candle. A chalice is set behind the unity candle with wine blessed by Leviathan. The bride and groom each are handed a burning wick to light their black candle and then together light the unity candle.

The Master or Mistress hands the chalice to the bride. She says "In the name of Lord Satan I drink this elixir to our everlasting union.". She then takes a sip from the chalice. The chalice is handed back to the Master or Mistress who then hands it to the groom. He repeats. The chalice is then handed back to the Master or Mistress and then placed upon the altar, behind the union candle.

The wine is now poured over the hands of the bride and groom and they are asked to face the east.

Master or Mistress

"In the name of Rosier, in the name of Mother Lilith, in the name of Lord Satan and all those who witnessed this today, you are now wed until the day you depart this physical world. Go to the East and Lucifer shall light your way."

The couple exits the circle to the East. The couple now keeps the cord as well as the remaining unity candle.

INITIATION RITUAL

The initiate enters the clearing where the adepts have gathered in a circle in the ritual area. They surround the initiate. The council stands behind the altar and the master and or mistress stands in front of the altar. The initiate kneels before the altar on both knees.

Master: Is your will true

Initiate: Yes, for my will is with Satan

Mistress: What is true

Initiate: There is no law, no authority, no justice. There is only Satan

Master: If asked to kill for your brother or sister will you raise your sword.

Initiate: Yes, I will kill for my brother or sister for Satan is in my heart

Mistress: Will you die for your brother or sister

Initiate: Yes, I will die for my brother or sister for Satan is in my heart

Master: Who is your guide to the unmanifested universe

Initiate: Satan is my guide and in him I trust

Mistress: And to whom do you devote yourself

Initiate: To Lord Satan

Now the initiate will take a piece of paper and on this paper there will be the symbol of the Lilin Society. He will make a small cut on his left thumb and drop blood upon it. He will hand it to the master and or mistress. They will take the paper and burn it upon the altar.

Master: This is your oath, your binding to our Sect and to Lord Satan. This is your oath of secrecy and if you break your oaths may your soul burn in the flames of hell's wrath

Initiate: I swear on my sinister honor as a Satanist in the Lilin Society that I will never surrender, that I will die fighting rather than submit to any mortal, even if that means taking my own life. I will uphold the code of sinister honor.

The initiate rises and is given a necklace with the sigil of the Lilin Society. This is to be worn under the clothing not visible to mundanes but may be worn outside the clothing within the Sect. He has now become an adept.

Upon the Death of a Master or Mistress

When a Master or Mistress of a sect dies or even just wishes to step down the other head will select a new one from the sect. For Example: If the Mistress dies and Master will select a new Mistress.

If the Sect has only one but not the other, such as a Master but no Mistress, then the council will vote upon who will take their place. Note that a dying Master or Mistress cannot choose their replacement for their mind is dying and their judgement cannot be trusted.

A funeral is held in the name of the departed Master of Mistress. The typical funeral rite is not conducted but a special one for Masters or Mistresses. Here follows that ritual.

Upon the altar is the casket of the departed (if no body could be obtained a picture of the deceased is fine). Behind the altar is the symbol of the Lilin Society and on the altar are black candles, one lit for every year the Master or Mistress has been alive. There are also red candles, one lit for every year that they served as Master or Mistress.

The Initiates enter first, each one carrying a rose. They walk by the casket and place the rose inside on top of the body. They then take a seat in the back row.

Next the Adepts enter and follow the lead of the Initiates. They take a seat in the middle rows.

Finally the Council enters and they follow the lead of the previous two and then take a seat in the front rows.

Initiates begin the chant by chanting "Sa-tan, Chav-a-joth, Lil-ith, Qay-in". Adepts follow after three verses with a low "om". The council follows after three verses with a higher "ah".

The Master or Mistress enters the room and all goes silent. They stand before the altar. They lean down and kiss the corpse on the head. He consecrates a circle. This is as follows.

Earth "Lirach tasa vefa wehlic, Belial"

Air "Renich tasa uberaca biasa icar, Lucifer" Fire "Ganic tasa fubin, Flereous" Water "Jedan tasa hoet naca, Leviathan" After this circle is consecrated

The Master then turns to the crowd.

Master: "_____ served us well as Master/Mistress. He/she never put the sect second, always taking the time to work with its members. He/she has served Lord Satan well during their time upon their Earth. May their evolved spirit escape rebirth and move forward into the Unmanifested Universe."

"I call upon Euronymous, I call upon Baalberith, I call upon Babael. I call upon these demons to see over this funeral and watch over the departed. Now we will all stand as each row comes up one at a time and places their departing notes into the burning bowl."

Each member beforehand had hand written a personal prayer for the deceased to be watched over. Starting with the Initiates and ending with the Council each member will pass by the body, depositing their note into a large metal bowl.

Now when all is seated the Master will read each note. When he is done he will say "By Flereous your spirit is lifted. In the sacred flames you shall rise." He will then burn the note, dropping it into a separate burning bowl.

The Master now lights incense and waves them over the casket.

Master: "By Lucifer your spirit settles and is released back into the Womb of Tiamat. Hail Chaos."

All: "Hail Satan"

Sand is then poured on the burnt letters.

Master: "By Belial you become one with him. May you find rebirth in Chaos."

A Chalice of consecrated water is poured.

Master: "By Leviathan your spirit is released. May you find rebirth in Chaos."

The sigil of the Patron demon of the deceased is now traced over the bowl with a wand.

Master: "May _____ guide you and watch over you."

Master: "In the name of Lord Satan it is done. We bid farewell to our brother/ sister."

Following is a banquet. If there is a living spouse of the deceased they sit at the head of the table.

Afterwards

This is all you need to get started creating your sect, running your sect and creating your Book of Ahriman. If you have any further questions feel free to email Asha'Shedim directly at his personal email:

entheogeniclab@gmail.com

As a final reminder; the password to the Esoteria section of the Lilin Society is to be given to NO ONE. Only I can give out the password but if you email me and tell me you have an adept I will more than likely take your word that he can be trusted with it without making him go through the initiation process.

PART SIX: BOOK OF INITIATION

The following is given to Initiates who wish to join the Sect. Some material is repeated to let you know that it belongs in the Initiation packet. This is the same material and test given to all members who wish to join the overall Lilin Society.

INTRODUCTION

I would like to applaud your decision to become a member of the Lilin Society. Whether you are a neophyte or an adept to the dark arts you will find plenty of information and rituals to aid you in your path to spiritual evolution. The burning path begins here with initiation. The purpose of initiation is to weed out the weekend Satanists, those whom use the term for fashion, shock or some other perversion. What we practice here in the Lilin Society is true sinister Gnostic based Satanism.

Are you new to Gnostic Satanism? If so read on and understand it and see if it speaks to your Azoth (spirit). Those who undertake the task of initiation are elevated among their peers for they show true devotion to the dark Lord Satan and the whole movement of Satanism.

We do not discriminate based on skin color or sexual orientation. Live by our sinister honor and we will accept you as a brother or sister. The mundane (non Satanist) is our enemy and we despise them indiscriminately but isn't it our misanthropy of the mundane world and our love for our own sinister kind that unites us?

If you read this book and the Lilin Society is not for you (and it is not for everyone) I understand. The tasks of becoming an elite are overwhelming to some, but the pain of evolution is minuscule to the rewards you shall reap.

Understand that we are no way affiliated with the Temple of the Black Light, in fact they look poorly upon the Lilin Society and see me, Asha'Shedim, as an enemy. This is due to the fact that I teach Satanic Gnosticism and they feel that they own all the rights to the religion. No one owns a religion, it is free for all to use.

Although we are not affiliated with the Order of the Nine Angles a lot of their teachings influence my work as I myself am a niner (a member who doesn't belong to a Sect and lives by the code of Sinister Honor).

It should also be mentioned that there exists many enemies of the Lilin Society, mainly hardcore supporters of the Temple of the Black Light. Being a member of the Lilin Society makes these enemies your enemies as well, for you carry the name of the Lilin Society. Although there has been no violence as of yet I feel as an initiate you should know what you are getting yourself into, what you are representing.

Now this brings the introduction to an end. When you are ready, read on.

Chaos

1. There was no beginning and there shall be no end. Lawlessness and Chaos is eternal, all encompassing and everlasting.

2. It was always here, it shall always be here. There is no destruction for chaos.

3. This is the Unmanifested Universe. It is ruled by a god of no name, a god un- known. Within the perfection of the acausal everything is possible for Chaos is perfect, the Unknown God is perfect.

4. There was Ain, the Nothingness of Divinity in all its wondrous Fullness of Emptiness. This was the true Holiness, the unlimited and unrestrictive.

5. In the beginning of slavery, creation, from chaos fell a small portion of Divine Chance. It fell down though the heart of nothingness and toward the Limit. Thus was created Ain Sof.

6. This was the non-limited but with it was carried limit caused by separation. Within this state of Ain Sof divinity was restricted by the unlimited yearning to learn limit. As the will of the Demiurge manifested, so did his opposition.

7. Half sought to further causality while the other aimed to uphold the Ain, acausality. One side was with thought of separation while the other was unwilling to know to avoid further restriction.

8. The Ain Sof was absolute, leaving no possibility of conflicting thought and thoughtlessness within it. Each side limited each other as one sought the path of restriction and the other wished to be absorbed back into the womb of Tiamat.

9. The void and empty space was produced by the retracting side of causal thought of creation while the thoughtless became further removed. To build manifestation the side of restriction became a Light with Limit. It shot down from the Tzimtzum and into the void of Tehiru, the void created by the opposing sides. Thus creation was formed.

10. Until this moment the thoughtless side was slumbering. Upon awakening it established its own force to counteract that of the light of creation and thus to limit the void where thoughtful light could shine.

11. The light of the causal had acquired the upper half of Tehiru while the acausal acquired the lower half. At the point where the two sides collided split bits of the two lights and engulfed each other. A gate formed causing an unwanted bounding in which one side is imprisoned the sparks of the Black Light while the other absorbed the white.

12. Thus the Tree of Life was created by Causal Light through ten emanations. The Demiurge would use this to limit and make himself known without Chaos.

13. The Acausal Light opposed the Cosmic Order. This was further instigated from the barriers of Tehiru as well as the sparks that were imprisoned within the Tree of Life.

14. The sparks immediately rebelled. The Cosmic further parted from Chaos and the Acausal Light became furious. Within the fourth emanation, known at that time as Masukhiel, the rebellion began. The trapped sparks took forms which threatened the will of the Demiurge. The leader of this first rebellion was the Prince of all warriors of the Acausal Light and his name was Qemetial.

15. The Demiurge handled the rebellion by destroying Masukhiel. The emanation absorbed Qemetial and his warriors. Although their forms were destroyed their essence continued on for their spirit was born out of Chaos.

16. The Demiurge made a second attempt to create the fourth emanation. More of the essence of the opposing side was trapped and the war continued. The leader this time was Belial. His warriors were more aggressive and attacked harder. The Demiurge again destroyed this sphere and the warriors but still their essence existed.

17. The sphere again formed, this time with even more opposition. Ruled by Athiel these warriors were fiercest of all with the sole ambition to destroy Cosmic Creation and reduce all back to the formless. Again Masukhiel was destroyed but the essence remained.

18. The Demiurge this time absorbed this Sephira's entire existence. He pushed it into the Other Side, creating the abyss Masak Mavdil. This was the place for Rejected Failures which became a pit leading to the Other Side.

19. To cover the wound on the Tree of Life Daath was created and placed upon the huge pit. This time it remained stable and the rest of the ten emanations were created.

20. The Acausal Light in its abysmal side in Tohu had kept its core essence of Ain beyond constrictive forms and connected it its source. In Bohu it had kept its spirit empty of all impulses with the exception of those who strive to return to Ain.

21. Now through Chasek it aimed to undo creation. Chasek mimicked the Ain Soph Aur. They took the form of an eleven headed dragon to fight creation. And this dragon is called Chavajoth.

22. The black serpents of the Other Side formed the adverse Tree of Death.

THE BOOK OF QAYIN AND LULUWA

1. Adam and Eve lived in the Garden of the Creator. This garden was the first tool of propaganda used to establish an ego ignorant of spirit. It was a garden of Sephirotic bondage. Adam was Clayborn, whereas Eve was Fireborn. Within the garden grew a strange tree which was black in color with black leaves and from this tree hung luscious fruit. The tree had its roots so deep that they reached Sitra Achra and served as a gateway between the world of creation and the Other Side. The Demiurge feared the power of this alien tree and forbade Adam and Eve to partake in its magnificent fruits.

2. Adam was made from the clay and thus was Clayborn. Eve came from Adam's rib and life was breathed into her from the Demiurge using stolen sparks from the Other Side. This made Eve fireborn for she was born from the acausal energy from the Other Side. The Gods of the other side saw this and felt empathy for Eve. Samael-Lilith decided to act and cross into the garden through the gateway tree.

3. The tree as called the Tree of Knowledge, for its fruits held the truth that the Demiurge hid from Adam and Eve. Samael-Lilith took the form of a serpent and crossed over.

4.Eve felt a detachment to the Demiurge and her Fireborn blood made her naturally dissident, however she was ignorant of the truth. She didn't have Gnosis. As the serpent descended down the black branches of the tree Eve immediately felt a warm attachment to the serpent for she sensed something of her own within it. Adam felt nothing. The serpent told her to eat of the forbidden fruit and defying the will of the Demiurge she did.

5. Adam was hesitant but the lusciousness of the fruit was too much to ignore and Adam joined Eve.

6. Eve began to understand as her spirit, Azoth, was awoken. She understood now for the first time the extent of her slavery for she had now the Black Flame burning within her. Adam saw nothing of the sorts and only saw his own nakedness. The serpent face of Lilith hypnotized Adam who fell into a trance and then eventually went to sleep.

7. Now Eve was alone with the serpent whom she felt affection for. The serpent of Samael-Lilith planted a seed in her womb and then retreated back to Sitra Achra.

8. Adam awoke and Eve proclaimed that the Lord had blessed her with child. Adam, feeling guilty for defying his God, went to the Demiurge and told him everything except for the pregnancy. The Demiurge became outraged. He ordered Adam and Eve to drink from the river of the lost, and much to Eve's desire to retain what she had learned; she obeyed and drank from the river, blinding the spirit that was in her. The seed, that of Samael-Lilith, was unaffected by the water. Adam and Eve were banished from the garden and sent to the cursed Earth.

9. The Earth was a horrid place of danger and ugliness. The seed in Eve grew and split into two fetuses. On the day that they were born they were one male and one female. Both babies were beautiful beyond words for they had Azoth within them. They were Fireborn and their names were to be Qayin and Luluwa.

10. Qayin and Luluwa became quite fond of each other. As children they were inseparable and their love for each other grew for they both had the spirit within them. Their blood burned but they didn't understand why for they had yet to discover the Black Flame within themselves.

11. Adam and Eve had a set of twins called Able and Aklia. They were Clayborn like their parents and unlike Qayin and Luluwa. Also unlike Qayin and Luluwa the Clayborn children were lazy and weak. Qayin tended to his crops while Luluwa tended to her garden. In secrecy they learned the art of Witchcraft using the acausal energy found in herbs. When Qayin tended to the soil it changed and grew beautiful crops. Where ever Luluwa went what was once ugly became beautiful and thus the cursed Earth began to flourish, influenced by their Azoth.

12. Because of the beauty of the Fireborn siblings, the Clayborn siblings seeked marriage with them. Able and Aklia went to their father and asked if they could marry their siblings. Able wished to marry Luluwa and Aklia wished to marry Qayin. Immediately Qayin and Luluwa opposed as they revealed their wish to marry each other. Adam opposed but decided to seek out the will of his God.

13. The Demiurge favored Adam but told Qayin and Able that he would decide after they made a sacrifice in his name, only then would he decide who would marry who. Able acted swiftly and sacrificed the first of his sheep flock. He burned the fat upon the altar and the smoke rose. The Demiurge accepted the sacrifice and was pleased. Qayin, whose blood burned with Azoth, didn't have the devotion to the Demiurge that Able had and thus his sacrifice was mere berries from his harvest. The Demiurge rejected the sacrifice and the smoke fell toward the Earth.

14. It was thus decided by the Demiurge that Able had won and Able was to marry Luluwa where Qayin was to marry Aklia. Able rejoiced and praised his creator whereas Qayin cursed him. As Able dropped to his knees before the Demiurge in praise Qayin stormed off. His blood felt something new, something which felt right. He felt wrath.

15. Qayin and Luluwa's love was genuine and both worked hard unlike their siblings. The Demiurge proved to be unfair for he rewarded the weak and punished the strong. Qayin and Luluwa discussed in great length as to what to do and it was decided that they would kill Able and Aklia.

16. Luluwa seduced Able easily and told him that she wanted him to take her to the fields where Qayin tended and take her as his wife there in the field. Able, overcome with blind lust, eagerly followed his sister to his own death.

17. Qayin waited in the field. When Luluwa and Able arrived Qayin stepped out of the shadows. Able cried out for mercy for he saw the wrath burning in his brother's eyes. Qayin killed Able without mercy.

18. The blood flowed toward the Earth and the Earth drank it up. Qayin felt an awakening as the Black Flame hidden within him awoken. He had reached Gnosis by being the first murderer and thus sealed his fate as the Lord of Death.

19. Qayin saw a raven and followed the raven to a spot in the field out in the open. Here he buried the first grave and the Earth accepted the sacrifice. Through the act of murder Qayin became the first Satanist.

20. Qayin seduced Aklia who eagerly followed him to Luluwa's beautiful garden with promise to make love. Luluwa, full of rage, stepped out from the

shadows and killed Aklia. She followed the act of Qayin and buried her, this time hidden beneath a rose bush.

Luluwa felt the Black Flame within and thus became the second Satanist.

21. When Able and Aklia never returned home Adam sought out the Demiurge. The Demiurge discovered the grave of Able for it was in an open field but never discovered the body of Aklia. The Demiurge made Qayin stand before him and proclaimed that the blood of Able cried out to him. The creator banished Qayin and Luluwa putting a curse on them and a mark on Qayin's head.

22. The two Satanists went out and formed their own kingdom named after their first son Enoch. Here they perfected the arts of Witchcraft and had more Fireborn children. The children of Adam and Eve feared the Qayin bloodline for they were Clayborn like their parents. Thus was the birth of Satanism.

THE ELEVEN STEPS TO HELL

Though my journey was long and harrowing I had reached the staircase and knew that I couldn't stop. I had to move forward. What stands at the right side of the staircase?

Asmodeus, the king of Demons.

Who stands at the left side of the staircase?

Astaroth, the prince of hell.

What do they each hold in their hands?

A pitchfork.

How many prongs are on the pitchfork?

Three.

What do the three prongs represent?

Mind, body and spirit.

What does the shaft represent?

Evolution.

What is in the sky?

A black hole.

What is the staircase railings made of?

Human bone.

What is on the first step?

A dead griffin, King of the Sky and King of the Land. It was killed by a serpent.

What is on the second step?

The daeva Aka Manah.

What is he holding?

A human skull

What is in the left socket?

A tigers eye stone.

What is in the right socket?

Obsidian

What is on the third step?

The goddess of death, Kali

What does she hold in her right hands?

Pitchforks

What does she hold in her left hand?

Severed heads of our enemies

What is on the fourth step?

A fetus hung from an umbilical cord noose.

What is on the fifth step?

A child sacrifice burning in the bull oven. The flames of Moloch cleanse it.

What is on the sixth step?

The faceless queen, Ama Lilith

What is on the seventh step?

Santa Muerte

What is in her left hand?

The scales

What is in her right hand?

The planet, showing death's domination on this planet.

What does her scythe symbolize?

Her reach.

What is on the eighth step?

The Zahhak, the massive dragon of Lord Ahriman.

What is on the ninth step?

Belphegore

What is his throne made of?

Human corpses.

What is on the tenth step?

Satan and Moloch

Who is looking up?

Satan, toward Chaos

Who is looking down?

Moloch, toward Sitra Achra

What is on the eleventh step?

The black flame

These are the Eleven Steps to Hell. Memorize them and keep them secret.

UNDERSTANDING THE ACAUSAL

The acausal world is separate from our causal world. Those who work within the art have various degrees of understanding it depending on their experience. The one thing all followers of the occult are in agreement on is that it does exist.

All life has acausal energy. This is not the same as the acausal spirit which only the Fireborn have. In our physical universe whether we are talking about rocks, planets, star systems or chemical compounds, they cannot move without physical or chemical assistance. Only life can move without any kind of outside assistance, and the reason for this is that our bodies are fueled with acausal energy, it is imported. Every living thing is a nexion, gateway, to the acausal realm for we must import it somehow.

Energy cannot be created nor can it be destroyed. The creator, the Demiurge, has placed our spirit, Azoth, within this biological body. He did not create us, just the physical world all around us.

Now in understanding sorcery we must understand the acausal energy and must accept the fact that we are a nexion. There are two main types of sorcery. There is endogenic sorcery (acausal) and exogenic (causal). The endogenic sorcery uses the acausal energy we import from our inner nexion. Exogenic sorcery is generated from the causal world all around us within the physical world.

The tools we use in ritual magic are simply to aid us in working with our inner consciousness, and that is it. The tools which work for one sorcerer may not be the same that works with another, but they are just physical things. Real skilled sorcerers will need no tools to achieve results for it all involves consciousness.

Ceremonial rituals (involving more than one person) are quite powerful for there are multiple minds and nexions channeling the energy but it is stressed that all participants must be adepts in their art and be on the same level of experience. The results of inexperienced working with adepts can be mentally catastrophic resulting in madness or even death.

In the acausal world there exist acausal entities. The demons and gods we work with and worship are acausal entities and to work with them one must understand their nature and how they exist. It would be sheer ignorance to view them from the perspective of our restrictive world. They are not bound by laws of time, travel, dimension etc. With this knowledge one can understand better how two or more people invoking the same entity may work. If a sorcerer in one part of the world is invoking a spirit while across the globe another is invoking the same spirit at that time, the entity can be in two places at once for in our world it is all encompassing. We are restricted to one place at a time, they are not.

Satan is real acausal entity. He is not a symbolism or an idea, he is real and he exists. He is the adversary of our cosmic creator and architect, the Demiurge. Dualism exists in this way, the restricting forces of Order and creation and the unbound and unmanifested realm of Chaos which existed long before Order. The Demiurge wishes to expand creation whereas Satan wishes to return all to chaos. This is why both entities have existed within the countless dualism religions over the years.

The ruler of all and god of chaos is the Unknown God. This is not to be confused with Satan or the Demiurge. Both are lesser entities. If we look at Zoroastrianism we can grasp this concept a little better. Zurvan can be compared to the Un- known god and from Zurvan came two entities, the God of Order and Cosmic Ahura Mazda and the God of Chaos and Anti-Cosmic, Angra Mainyu. Ahrura Mazda wishes to continue and grow creation whereas Angra Mainyu wishes to stop it.

Now in the discussion of death one can come to the following conclusion. Death is the physical expiration of the biological physical body, but our acausal spirit continues on after death. Where does it go from there? There are many theories but I subscribe to the idea of rebirth. The human body is equipped with a soul, an ego and in the case of the Fireborn, a spirit or Azoth. The ego is the chains which bound us to this cosmic prison. It keeps the spirit and soul stuck in the vicious cycle of rebirth and prevents our return to the acausal realm.

How this works is through anchors, our attachment to this world. The more we surround ourselves with materials the more anchors we develop. When the ego dies a new ego is made in which the soul and or spirit is again attached to it. The problem is when we die and our ego dies we lose all knowledge and experiences we acquired in our previous life. Only the deeply rooted gnosis of the Azoth carries on but we must work to acquire gnosis.

How we return to the Other Side is through limiting our anchors and practicing spiritual segregation. We must train ourselves to not over indulge, to not become attached to this world and to accept that it is all an illusion, to strengthen our Azoth and thus defeat our ego once and for all. The ego is how the Demiurge controls us and strengthens Creation.

Satanism can then be understood as a mechanism of evil, one with a goal to destroy Creation and return all to the acausal world. From a personal level, we practice endogenic sorcery to acquire gnosis and from a collective level we practice aeonic sorcery to strengthen the currents to aid in the total destruction of this world all around us.

GODDESS OF DEATH

1. Kali is time and nothing can escape the storm of time.

2. She is the great Goddess of Death, a good death. She aids in the destruction of the false ego as she separates the illusion from the Azoth. She brings the cleansing death to help aid us in understanding.

3. Her home is the holy cremation grounds. Go to cremation grounds and meditate.

4. Overcome the I-am-the-body attitude. The body is a vessel to seat the spirit. It is temporary. Never forget this.

5. Cremate the body that feeds the ego. Let the flames of Kali burn the flesh and liberate.

6. She is the great mother and we are her children. She is the liberator. She is the destroyer of the illusion of reality. The ego fears Kali because when the ego stares at Kali it sees its demise. It sees the killer of egos.

7. You who are attached to the ego, you see not a liberator but a demon. See only terror and fall victim to her fearsome form.

8. Garland of skulls and skirt of severed arms, these are symbolic of the death of ego for the ego arises from the body. Sever the body from the spirit and the ego will die. The garland and the skirt are trophies of her children she has liberated, torn the screaming ego from their body.

9. Her skin is dark for it represents the womb of Tiamat, the unmanifested reality from which the acausal originate, and to where all creation will eventually decay.

10. Kali is calm for she is blissful in her consciousness, free of her ego. Let the Goddess of Death show you to the cremation grounds.

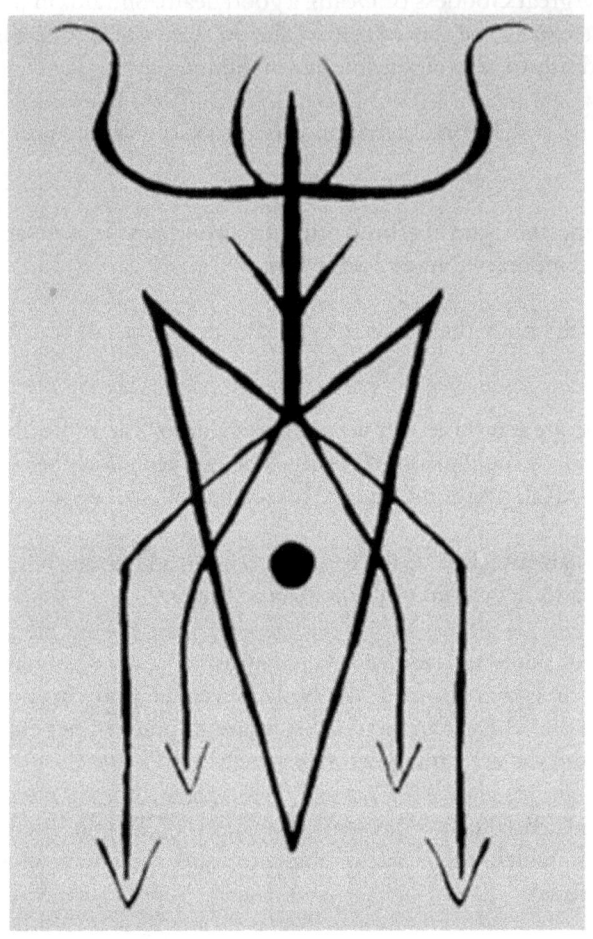

OUR SACRED SIGIL

Our sacred sigil was created by Lilin Society member Edgar Kerval, owner of Sirius Limited Esoterica publishings. This sigil first appeared on the cover of the limited production book "The Sinister Aeon" and has since been adopted as our sigil. As Edgar Kerval explained the sigil it is representing the acausal energies of the void and the Quimbanda astral temples. This sigil is our most sacred of symbols and a great gift of an important member.

THE TEST

Please fill out all requirements of the tests and email them to entheogeniclab@gmail.com with the subject reading INITIATION Understand that submission does not guarantee membership.

Please do the following tasks to join.

1. Read the Materials in this book
2. Complete test which follow
3. Essay on why you wish to join the Lilin Society and also about your experience level and a little about yourself. (Don't let experience level discourage you, we accept neophytes)

After this is done email the package to the Lilin Society. If you are approved you will be contacted shortly after.

OATH

I am a Satanist. I am a personification of the adversary of the Demiurge, a Fireborn serpent with the black flame burning within. I join the Lilin Society to evolve and to help my brothers and sisters evolve. I understand that my oath binds me to secrecy and I swear to never reveal the secrets of the Lilin Society. In the name of Satan, ruler of Sitra Achra, in the name of the Unknown God, ruler of the Unmanifested Universe, I shall live by the Satanic Points and shall protect the secrecy of the Lilin Society.

Test

1. Who are the first Satanists?
2. What is acausal Energy?
3. Why is every person a Nexion?
4. What is Fireborn?
5. What is Clayborn?
6. What is the Chavajoth?
7. What is the Demiurge?
8. Who rules the unmanifested universe?
9. Who were the warriors of Masukhiel?
10. Who is Satan?
11. Define Satanism

ASHA'SHEDIM

Originally from Brockton Massachusetts, Asha'Shedim was born into a Catholic Italian family. At an early age he felt a disgust towards religion and grew a fascination for the One they preached in Sunday school as the root of all evil, Satan. Asha'Shedim's formative years were spent studying the occult in all its various manifestations.

In 2005 Asha'Shedim (then working under the name Aka Paimon) formed the Church of Luciferian Light, although he found it difficult to seek-out and unite like-minded individuals.

Once he disbanded the Church of Luciferian Light, he moved on to create the more esoteric and secretive Sect of Angra Mainyu. After a falling out with the council, the group fell apart and Asha'Shedim went into solitary practice once more. During this time he was heavily influenced by the Order of the Nine Angles and decided to bring his take on Gnostic Satanism public again with the creation of the Lilin Society in 2013. He has since written many books on the occult including the Grimoire of Asha'Shedim, the Tome of the Lilin Society and the Book of Ahriman.

Asha'Shedim has served in the United States Army National Guard as a means of an insight role, and has chosen career paths to follow this pathei-matho. He currently resides in North Carolina and presides over the Lilin Society from there.

www.lilinsociety.com

www.ingramcontent.com/pod-product-compliance
Lightning Source LLC
Chambersburg PA
CBHW071719090426
42738CB00009B/1816